The Art
and Science of
Metal
Detecting

Vince Migliore

Blossom Hill Books

Title ID 5726666

Title: **The Art and Science of Metal Detecting**

Description: *The Art and Science of Metal Detecting* is a user guide to choosing, understanding, and operating a metal detector.

ISBN-13:
978-1517255107

ISBN-10:
1517255104
Primary Category: Sports & Recreation / General

Country of Publication: United States
Language: English
Search Keywords: metal detecting, treasure hunting
Author: Vince Migliore
Blossom Hill Books
113 Sombrero Way
Folsom, California 95630 USA
Reorder: https://www.createspace.com/5726666

Blossom Hill Books

Table of Contents

Cover photo: The diagram illustrates the electrical function of the detector when it finds a coin. When there is no target in the detector's field then the pick-up coil receives only a weak signal in phase with the transmit coil. When the field crosses over a coin or any metal object the detector field generates an eddy current in the target. This in turn produces a small field which opposes the detector coil field, causing a phase shift in the waveform. The amount of phase shift helps identify the target.

Phase shift is explained with other illustrations in Appendix B starting on page 187.

1. Introduction

A. Welcome

Welcome to the fabulous world of metal detecting!

This is an adventure-filled hobby where you can find coins, jewelry, historic relics and precious metals. You can help people find their lost rings and even help police in forensic discovery. The hobby goes by various names – treasure hunting, dirt fishing, metal detecting, or coin-shooting. You'll have loads of fun and you can easily find enough valuables to pay for your detector.

The thrill of finding treasure is addictive. Every time that beep goes off in your headphones it's like getting a free pull on a slot machine handle. Will it be a jackpot or junk? Modern metal detectors have discriminators – a word you will soon become familiar with – which tells if that beep is for a real coin, or just a bottle cap.

Although the search for easy treasure might be the motivating factor when you start the hobby, you will soon recognize and appreciate the many rewards of this sport. You will learn how metal detectors work, which delves into physics, electricity, and electronics. You will learn about history, geology, and geography. Hiking over hill and dale, you will learn a lot about nature, and get plenty of exercise in the process. You will see birds and animals, trees and rivers, rocks and clouds. When you dig, you will discover mud and bugs, gems and jewelry, coins and relics.

Looking for places to search, and seeking help from other people, you will become involved in all aspects of social behavior. You will learn about the history of your town, talk with property owners, and become familiar with grounds-keepers. Best of all, you will find that people are kind, helpful, and generous. This is particularly true of metal detecting club members, who will help you to learn about the sport, and guide you on your way. Best of all, you will very quickly learn to discover hidden coins and treasure, just waiting at your feet. You will carry them home, sort them out, and enjoy the wealth gained from your efforts. Metal detecting is an awesome combination of learning, adventure, exercise, and gathering treasure. So, welcome to the sport!

B. Guaranteed success

This is not your daddy's metal detector! The old machines would beep at finding anything made of metal. Today's detectors have electronic circuitry that <u>guarantees you will find valuables</u>.

The technology is called "discrimination" – something we will discuss later on – that *identifies the object in the ground even before you start digging!* This makes it possible to dig only the worthwhile finds and speeds up the treasure collection process.

Discrimination (the positive meaning of that word) allows Target Identification – the ability to tell the difference between a quarter and a bottle cap, between a penny and a dime, or between any coin and a piece of junk. The detector can tell you if it's a penny, a quarter, a dollar coin or precious metal. In this way, you can eliminate the long process of digging only to find it's a metal washer and not a coin. See Figure 1.

Modern detectors often have built-in pin-pointers to help you zero in on the exact location. Many will tell you how many inches deep it is too. All you do is swing the detector, read the display, and you make the choice to dig it up or not.

In a nutshell, the modern metal detector is a money-making machine. The ability to discriminate between buried coins and plain old trash enables you to retrieve valuables at a much faster rate than the old-timers did.

Figure 1. A modern metal detector can identify which coin it is sensing. Here a White's detector shows an ID number 18, indicating a 5-cent coin or a ring.

C. Essential strategy

A quick overview:

1. Above all else, you must understand the concepts of Discrimination and Target ID in order to evaluate which detector is best for you. These technical terms are defined in Chapter 3, *The Science of the Metal Detector*.

2. Next, it's advisable to know which types of metal detecting are available in your area. If you live in Oregon, for example, you may not be looking for Civil War relics. This topic is also covered in Chapter 3.

3. Finally, consider your budget and activity level. You don't want to spend a small fortune on a detector just to see it collect dust in your garage. Costs and trade-offs are discussed in Chapter 4, *The Art of Choosing a Detector*.

D. Detecting research

In this book you will learn how to:

- Choose the best detector for your needs
- Find the types of detecting (coins, jewelry, relics, gold prospecting) best suited for your area
- Find clubs, friends, and metal detecting resources
- Locate the hot search sites for your town
- Research local history that will point towards long-forgotten search areas
- Discover old maps and references to help locate good places to hunt
- Examine your target area from birds-eye and street level views to choose the best approach for metal detecting.

Most of the research can be completed with a few mouse clicks on the internet. As an example, you might be looking for old campgrounds. The internet has plenty of auction sites where you can buy reference guides to campsites in your area from the 1960s. You can buy one for about $5.00 on Ebay.com. Compare it to a modern map and you will see which campgrounds are still around and which have been abandoned or built over. Then use sites such as Google Earth or Panormaio.com to look at photos of these areas. They might be in a state park that charges a parking fee, but the aerial map shows an entrance from a residential area that is free. Study the online maps and even before you get there you know exactly what the terrain looks like and where you'll go to search.

E. The metal detector

The main piece of equipment you will need is a metal detector. This is composed of an electronic control box that processes the signal and gives you signal that you've located a metal object. The output can be a sound, a reading on a volt-meter, a display of a number on an LCD screen, or any combination of such methods. The detector will also have a grip and arm-rest, and a shaft to hold the search coil. The sound output goes to a speaker which is usually bypassed by plugging in a set of headphones. See Figure 2.

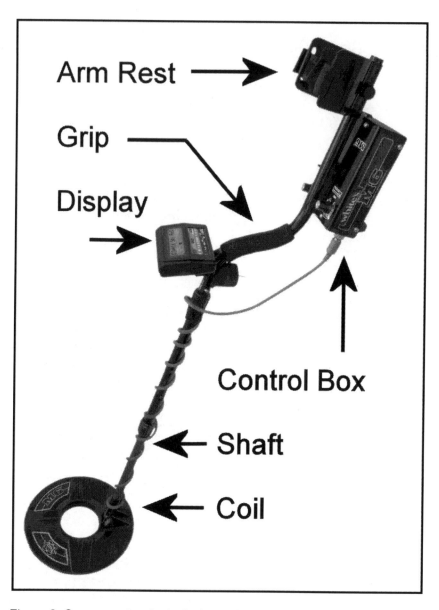

Arm Rest →

Grip

Display

Control Box

← Shaft

← Coil

Figure 2. Components of a typical metal detector. Some detectors have a control box with no display, and use different pitch sounds to identify the target. For other detectors the display is integral to the control box.

You turn the detector on, adjust a couple of dials, put on the headphones, and you're ready to go. You move the detector coil across the ground in a slow, sweeping motion until you get a "hit." Depending on the output from the control box you can tell if you have a coin or a piece of junk. Some detectors use a high pitched tone for good targets and a low frequency grunt for junk. Others have an icon or LCD display which tells you what the target is likely to be. This saves a lot of time digging.

Extra equipment, such as a pin-pointer, a probe, and a tool belt, makes retrieving your finds much easier. This book explains how to select a metal detector, and contains a brief description of the equipment involved in metal detecting, as well as resources for further research.

Figure 3. Every outing results in finding at least some coins.

F. Code of ethics

The following Code of ethics is reprinted from *Western & Eastern Treasures* magazine.

Treasure Hunter's CODE OF ETHICS

- I WILL respect private property and will do no treasure hunting without the owner's permission.
- I WILL refill all excavations.
- I WILL appreciate and protect our heritage of natural resources, wildlife, and private property.
- I WILL use thoughtfulness, consideration and courtesy at all times.
- I will build fires in designated or safe places only.
- I WILL leave gates as found.
- I WILL remove and dispose of any and all trash and litter that I find.
- I WILL NOT litter.
- I WILL NOT destroy property, buildings, or what is left of ghost towns and deserted structures.
- I WILL NOT tamper with signs, structural facilities, or equipment.

2. What's It All About? A Typical Day

What is a typical metal detecting adventure all about, anyway?
Come along as we go "dirt fishing" to a local site. Everything
that happens in this real-life expedition will tie in to one of the
chapters that follow in the book.

A. Metal detecting equipment

A seasoned detector enthusiast may have put in a lot of thought
into choosing the right metal detector. He's been coin hunting for
a while now, and he's chosen a name brand manufacturer with a
good reputation. It's not the cheapest metal detector, nor is it the
most expensive. It's a nice combination of features that are
helpful in this particular part of the country. The detector has
Target Identification, adjustable discrimination, and variable
sensitivity.

Many detectorists keep their gear in a tidy box in the back of the
car. The coil also requires some thought. If it's too small you
won't get the depth you need to find those long-lost treasures,
and if it's too big, swinging it around all morning is going to tire
out your arms. You may also want an old but functional leather
tool belt, which serves as a carrier for all the probes and diggers.
The belt stores the junk in one pouch, and coins in the other.

Read more about selecting the right equipment in *The Science of the Metal Detector*, Chapter 3, *The Art of Choosing a Detector*, Chapter 4, and *Related Detecting Equipment*, Chapter 5.

The back of the car has a few digging tools and an old pair of boots used only for metal detecting. There's a bunch of extra batteries for the equipment. Another essential is a good hand-held pin-pointer for zeroing in on those elusive treasures. Many of the coins turn reddish brown after living underground for decades, and the hand-held pin-pointer makes short work of distinguishing coins from clods of dirt. Some enthusiasts also take a sports jar full of water, a camera, and a towel.

B. Choosing a location

Choosing the right place to hunt is part of the essential preparation for metal detecting. The area we have in mind for today's hunt is a large lot of empty land owned by the city. It runs parallel to one of the oldest streets in town. This location is on a main thoroughfare created before the interstate highway was built back in the 1950s. How do I know? I searched the internet for an antique map of the city. For $5.00 I now have a map that shows which parks and schools were around in the '50s, and which roads were heavily used then. That's called research and planning. See also: *The Art of the Hunt,* Chapter 6.

It's hard to say when the research and planning for a treasure hunt really starts. That's because, like a photographer, you learn to keep an eye out for good locations. Just driving down the street you might notice big old trees and undeveloped land. This is a sure sign that the territory has remained untouched for over 50 years. Key things to look for are old trees, property that is free of landscaping, and places that had foot traffic in the past. It helps to get up early for a hunt. That helps to avoid large crowds or events that might interfere with the coin-shooting.

C. The people you meet

Before I drive out to the site, I give my buddy a call to let him know I'm on the way. He is a member of the metal detecting club I joined. Having him as a treasure hunting companion has really helped. Not only is he more experienced than I am, but he's helped steer me to the right books, maps, and magazine articles that have improved my skills. Besides, you don't want to be alone in some back-woods area if you fall or need help of some kind. Such friends have taught me how to approach land owners and utility people to gain their permission to search specific sites.

Joining a metal detecting club is probably the best choice you can make for enjoying this sport. People in these organizations are cooperative, knowledgeable, and full of stories that will make you smile. The club organizes group hunts, annual events, and monthly meetings. Learn more about *Hunting for People,* Chapter 7.

D. Metal detecting techniques

I get to the search site, and my friend is already there. I get my tool belt on and load it up with a digging tool, the pin-pointer, and a towel to wipe my hands. I turn on the metal detector, and adjust it for ground conditions at this site. The detector has a discrimination control and Target Identification (TID). The TID numbers tells me if the beep in the headphones is from a dime or a bottle cap, and it displays a message to that effect on a small screen built into the housing. Some detectors use the term VDI, for Visual Discrimination Indication, to identify targets. The discriminator allows me to adjust the detector so that there is no beeping sound when I swing it over a pull-tab from a soda can, but that also causes me to miss out on certain treasures, such as silver rings.

Figure 4. In this hobby you learn a lot from your friends.

I generally hunt with a buddy. Before we start searching, we both size up the site. There are some old trees, and a dirt pathway next to the road. This is a good site that has remained unchanged in many years. There is also a shortcut through the lot, which is well worn with lots of foot traffic. My friend starts searching by the trees, and I take to searching the pathway across the lot.

Right away the detector starts to beep, and the display shows a bottle cap, so I skip it. A minute later I get a hit for a dime. I crisscross the site with the coil, pressing the button for the pin-pointing function built into the detector. I memorize the spot as I lean over with the hand-held pin-pointer. This hand-held probe is so powerful I can often locate the coin even before I start digging. The metal detector shows that the coin is only one inch deep. I get out my digging tool, a screw driver in this case, and stab at the dirt. Right away the dime pops out. I search for the date. A dime minted before 1965 is silver – much more valuable. Whoops, too bad! This one is 1972. I continue scanning. In the first 10 minutes I retrieve 6 coins. This is a good site. Many of the coins are old, from the1970s, so there is a good chance of finding silver here. I find a broken watch too, and a token from a game arcade. The site yields a coin every few minutes.

Read more on *Metal Detecting Technique,* Chapter 8.

E. Science and skills

As I'm searching, I'm thinking of all the physical sciences that contribute to a good hunting trip. I can estimate the age of the trees to tell me how long this area has been vacant. See Figure 5. The weather is good. The soil is loamy with some clay, and it's easy to dig. There are no overhead power lines to interfere with the electronics. The coil size works well for the depth of coins I'm finding. Best of all, the history research and map planning paid off. I come away with 26 coins for two hours of searching, and I find lots of artifacts. It pays to do the research and understand the many disciplines involved with this hobby: geology, biology, history, and electronics. *Science and Your Hobby* is discussed in Chapter 9.

Figure 5. Being able to judge the age of an old tree will help in analyzing a search site. You will find other sciences aid in your evaluation of places to hunt.

F. Sorting and saving your finds

The coins go in one pouch on the tool belt, and the jewelry, tokens, and semi-precious junk go into a different compartment. This is the first phase of sorting and storing my finds. When I get home I wash them, sort them into separate containers and drawers that I have set up. In the garage is the big stuff – iron machinery, tools, and farming equipment. In the bottom drawer are the glass jars that hold the various coins. One is for "clad" pennies; those minted after 1981, which are mostly zinc. One is for real copper pennies, and one is for all the nickels, dimes, and quarters. For the really rare stuff I have separate little jars labeled with their contents. Every detectorist knows that in 1965 the US switched to plated coins, going off the silver standard. This makes finding dimes and quarters minted before 1965 especially precious. Those minted after 1965 are called "clad" coins and are

16

not as valuable. The real silver coins have their own special
containers.

Finally, there is a drawer for all the historical artifacts I find,
such as bullets, buckles, and buttons. When I accumulate enough,
I might sell them on Ebay. For more on *Caring for Your
Treasures*, see Chapter 10.

G. Prospecting

I enjoy searching on relatively flat land for coins, jewelry and
relics. Many people involved in metal detecting however like to
specialize in specific types of searches, such as looking for Civil
War artifacts. Others prefer beach hunting.

One of the major specialties in treasure hunting is prospecting for
gold, silver, or other precious metals. Gold prospecting in
particular is highly specialized. It uses equipment very similar to
detectors made for coin hunting, but the electronics may be
qualitatively different. Gold prospecting often involves
machinery unique to the hobby, such as dredging equipment and
sluice boxes. This is true also for meteorite hunting. For more on
Prospecting, see Chapter 11.

H. Growing into the hobby

Later that same week I attend our club meeting. Getting together with other metal detecting enthusiasts provides an opportunity to share stories, compare notes, and display what we've found. Even newcomers to the sport have experiences to share. It's not too long before you learn some special techniques that work well in your area. As you gain more knowledge you graduate from the novice level. See *Mastering Metal Detecting,* in Chapter 12.

I. Metal detecting resources

With the development of the internet, knowledge about metal detecting has grown by leaps and bounds. To keep up with this flood of information you will need to know something about *Metal Detecting Resources,* which are presented in **Appendix A.** This includes a list of the most popular web sites and magazines.

Appendix B explains *How a Detector Works.* **Appendix C** lists *Manufacturers and Suppliers.* **Appendix D** provides a *Checklist* for comparing detectors. Finally, if you get lost or want to look something up, there is a complete **Index** to subjects at the end of the book.

3. The Science of the Metal Detector

A. The value of discrimination

The modern metal detector uses electronic circuitry to locate metallic objects in the ground. The signal picked up by the detector coil is processed to help you tell the difference between junk and valuable metal or coins. This ability to distinguish trash from coins is called **Discrimination**. The quality and acuity of the discrimination enables **Target Identification** (TID). This is generally presented in a display that shows pennies, nickels, dimes, using icons.

An inexpensive metal detector might have only three levels of discrimination, which would be able to tell a penny from a metal washer, but it may not be able to tell the difference between a penny and a dime. An expensive detector has a higher level of discrimination ability and often uses Target ID numbers. These TID numbers are specific enough to tell the difference between a clad penny (a mostly zinc coin minted after 1981) and a copper penny. See Figure 6 for an example of these identification numbers (sometimes called VDI numbers). In Figure 6 the detector indicates it has found a penny or a dime. Sometimes the detector cannot tell exactly what coin it has found, but by studying the numbers you learn that a 79 is usually a penny, and an 81 is usually a dime. That is the power of good discrimination!

B. How discrimination works

How does discrimination work?

The detector coil works both as a transmitter and a receiver. The coil is energized by electricity. There are two basic laws of electricity that come into play in allowing the circuitry to identify a coin.

- The first law is that an electric current running through a wire generates a magnetic field around the wire.

- The second law is that a magnetic field cutting across a wire generates an electric current in that wire. It doesn't matter if the wire is moving through the field or the field is moving across the wire. In both cases there is a current induced in the wire.

When the magnetic field from the energized coil of the metal detector crosses over a coin, there is a slight, but measurable, current induced into the coin. The field in the coil is alternating current, usually between 5 khz and 10 khz. This alternating current generates a field that is continuously developing and collapsing around the coil. This creates a moving field that cuts across the coin in the ground. (Remember that second law, above!)

The coin is not a wire. It is a flat disk. It does, however, act like a very short wire. The induced current has nowhere to go, so it bounces around inside and along the surface of the coin. These are called eddy currents.

The eddy currents, although somewhat chaotic, generate a small magnetic field around the coin. (Remember the first law, above!) This field is then picked up by the detector coil.

If the coin is a silver dime, the currents can move pretty easily along the coin, since silver is an excellent electrical conductor. Further, all silver dimes are about the same size and thickness. The dime then has a distinctive "signature" that is picked up by the detector. Unless the dime is bent or severely corroded, this signature will be similar no matter its orientation below ground.

A nickel, compared to a dime, is larger and the metal is not as conductive. The currents in a nickel move slower and have more resistance to current flow. This generates a different electrical signature.

The metal detector processor then looks at the characteristics of the return signal bouncing off the coin and compares it to the known signatures of typical coins. If it's a close match to the standard dime signature, the detector will identify it as a dime and display the results. This is Target Identification!

Likewise, there are standard signatures for other size coins, bottle caps, pull tabs, aluminum foil, and other junk; Figure 6.

Jewelry, however, poses problems for the detector. A jewelry item can be large or small; it can be made of gold, silver, or a base metal; and it can be solid like a pendant or ring-shaped. The detector can make a good approximation of the value of the jewelry item based on its conductivity. Gold and silver, as mentioned, are excellent conductors of electricity, and this produces a faster, stronger response in the detector.

Relic hunting is another matter altogether. Relics, such as bullets or belt buckles, can be made of base metal, and may therefore have low conductivity. They may register low on the discrimination scale. If you are hunting in a Civil War battlefield, you will probably want to dig up everything, even what appears to be junk on the detector display.

In summary, the modern detector can recognize the size, the conductivity, and the strength of the signal bouncing off an object underground. It uses this information to give you a relatively reliable estimate of exactly what lies below the surface.

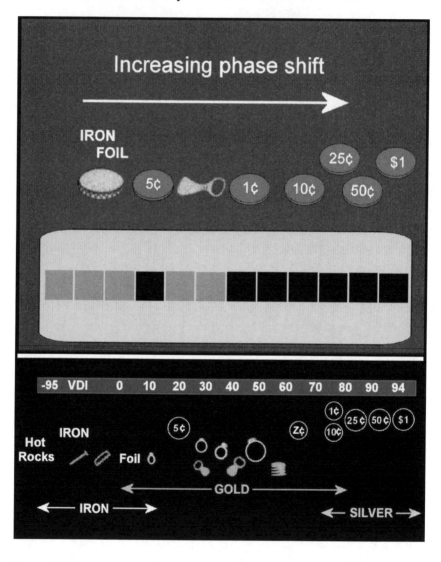

Figure 6. Examples of the discrimination displays for two different detectors. Top image shows a 12 notch scale as on the Garrett Ace 250. The lower image shows a VDI scale, -95 to +95, which has higher resolution.

C. Before you buy a detector

Your most important purchase will be the metal detector. Don't make the mistake of a hasty choice. You may end up with a detector that is a mismatch for your interests and for your location. If you plan to make an informed decision on which machine to buy, you will need:

> **FIRST** – Consider what is possible in your area. For example, if you live in the middle of the Nevada desert, you probably would not be choosing underwater equipment or be looking for Civil War relics. You are more likely to be successful at coin-shooting, searching for jewelry, or prospecting.

> **SECOND** – Study how detectors work. This subject is covered in **Section F** of this chapter. VLF detectors are by far the most common, but be aware of the newer Pulse Induction detectors. Study the brand names and their advertisements in hobbyist magazines.

> **THIRD** - become familiar with some of the tech-talk and key words which refer to functions of the machine, then decide if you really need them for your particular type of detecting. The key concept in metal detecting is the quality of discrimination, which allows you to identify objects in the ground. See **Section G** which follows.

Figure 7. The display panel from the Teknetics Omega detector shows words you need to understand before you buy a detector - - terms such as Target ID, Sensitivity, and Discrimination.

CAUTION: Take your time in choosing the right detector for your needs. This is usually a balance between you desire for effective technology and your budget constraints.

Figure 8. Metal detecting is often a social event, as in this beach hunt. Image courtesy of Garrett Electronics.

If you have the advantage of a friend who already owns a detector, then you will be ahead of the game. Arrange for a demonstration and instructions on how to use it. No matter how much you read, nothing can replace the hands-on experience of actually swinging a detector and hearing the sounds that indicate you've located a coin. Most dealers would be glad to demonstrate different machines too. Try it!

D. Detecting possibilities in your area

Metal detecting encompasses three broad but overlapping categories. These are land-based coin, jewelry, and relic hunting; beach, surf, and underwater detecting: and prospecting for gold, silver, and other metals. The general purpose detector will allow you to cover all three areas, but with some compromises. For example, the coil and shaft may be submersible in water, but not the control box.

<u>1. On-land coins and relics</u>

On-land detecting is the most common. Land-based metal detecting recovers coins, jewelry, tokens, household items, and historic relics. Most manufacturers focus on detectors for this purpose. Some brands produce detector models that have multiple modes, so they can search on land as well as in other environments. Land-based detecting includes cache hunting, which is the search for large amounts of stored treasure, such as a jar full of coins.

<u>2. Beach, surf, and underwater detecting</u>

Beach and underwater detecting requires a bit more specialized equipment due to the electrical properties of salt and water, and the need for water-proofing. The presence of salts and certain minerals requires some fine tuning for the detector to be able to see coins in this environment. The coil and shaft of such detectors are waterproof, while some are completely submersible for underwater detecting. Consider this specialty if you live near lakes, beaches, or large bodies of water.

Figure 9. Gold prospecting is limited to certain regions of the United States. The image of the lone prospector was made famous by the 1849 Gold Rush in California.

3. Prospecting for gold, silver, or other metals

Metals, minerals, and gold in particular, have distinct electrical properties. Metal detectors used for prospecting benefit from dedicated circuit design, which takes advantage of these properties. Operating frequencies are usually higher for prospecting than for on-land treasure hunting As with water detecting, salts and minerals are often encountered during prospecting, which requires a robust ground balancing system.

Many manufacturers produce multi-mode detectors which can operate across two or more of the environments listed above. Some models have a simple toggle switch which allows the operator to choose between coin, beach, or prospecting mode. Some hobbyists like to specialize in just one type of detecting, and will prefer to buy a detector that is dedicated to that mode. A person living along the coast in Florida, for example, may prefer a model that is dedicated to beach and surf detecting.

Meteorite hunting represents yet another variant in metal detecting. While you might find meteorites with pretty much any metal detector, those who want to specialize in this elusive search will often prefer to purchase or even construct specifically engineered detectors.

E. The basic technologies

1. First-generation technology

Beat-frequency oscillator (BFO) detectors are rare, older, and out of favor. You might still find such detectors available from old-timers or on the internet. They may work well enough for a beginner, but they do not have the advanced features found in modern detectors.

2. Very-low frequency (VLF) technology

The VLF detector is by far your best choice for most circumstances. VLF detectors feature **Discrimination**, which helps you distinguish between different coins and trash. Discrimination in turn enables **Target Identification**, which will tell you that you most likely have a nickel, a dime, a pull-tab, or whatever. The technology, sometimes referred to as induction-balance, is well-proven and popular with hobbyists. See **Appendix B** for a description on how it works.

3. Pulse induction (PI) technology

Pulse induction is a relatively new technology, but it is growing rapidly in popularity. This type of detector turns the search coil on for a fraction of a second. The same coil that sent the signal then listens for an echo from the target area. PI technology has the advantage of being better suited for difficult soil conditions, such as high salt or mineralization. This makes PI detectors more suitable for detecting gold, beach, and underwater applications. It has a drawback of poor performance in discriminating junk from valuable targets.

There are a few new technologies on the horizon, but few have yet to make their way into mainstream production. The following is quoted from Serious Detecting (http://www.seriousdetecting.com/library/metal-detector-technologies):

> "BBS (Bro"BBS (Broad Band Spectrum) simultaneously transmits, receives and analyzes a broad band of multiple frequencies to deliver substantial detection depth, high sensitivity and accurate discrimination for a wide range of target types. This broad band of frequencies provides the detector's electronics with more information about a target and the surrounding environment than is possible with single frequency technologies. The detector carries out advanced signal processing of these frequencies resulting in improved target identification accuracy and increased depth."

The geology of the area in which you live will have a major influence on the kind of detecting you are capable of. If you live in a state where gold deposits exist, for example, you might want to consider a model that is capable of prospecting.

F. Crucial concepts in detector operation

The **Key Words** you should become familiar with are explained below. They are:
- Discrimination and notch filtering
- Target Identification and VDI numbers
- Sensitivity
- Search depth
- Ground balance
- Operating frequency, or multiple frequencies

1. Discrimination and notch filtering

Discrimination is the ability of the detector to distinguish between one target and another. In most cases this translates into being able to distinguish between a coin and trash, such as between a quarter and a bottle cap. The composition of the object being scanned has an effect on the signal received by the metal detector. This effect is called **Phase Shift**. A positive, or leading, phase shift indicates a highly conductive target, such as a silver dime. A negative, or lagging, phase shift generally indicates junk, such as a rusty nail. An adjustable discrimination dial lets the operator tune out and reject signals from the junk targets.

The discriminator dial, in effect, blocks any response from the detector for targets with a phase shift at or below the level you select. Unfortunately, when you tune out the pull-tabs from soda cans you also tune out nickels and some jewelry. Experience adjusting the discriminator setting then becomes an important part of the learning curve for the novice coin-shooter. Some advanced metal detectors (more expensive) let you tune out only certain portions of the phase shift spectrum. This is called **Notch Filtering**. For example, you could tune out most of the pull tabs and still get nickels with careful notch filtering.

As you might guess, discrimination is extremely valuable in the field, where you don't want to spend a lot of time digging up garbage. In some situations, such as relic hunting, discrimination might not be as crucial, since relic hunters will often choose to dig up everything made of metal.

2. Target Identification (TID)

Target Identification is closely related to discrimination. Modern discriminating metal detectors can tell you if the target is a copper penny (minted before 1982) or a zinc penny. It can tell between a silver dime (minted before 1965), and what we call a "clad" dime, one that is a composite of copper and nickel. See **Figures 10** and **11**, below, for examples.

The output of the discrimination circuitry can be an audible tone, with a high pitched tone for valuables and a low grunt for junk. This is called **Tone Identification**. The output is more commonly a meter reading, or a numeric value called a VDI number which appears on a screen. VDI stands for Visual Discrimination Indicator. Discrimination output sometimes uses multiple modes to alert the operator. A high-pitched tone will indicate a high-conductivity target, while the LDC display shows both a VDI number and a probable target. On White's metal detector, for example, a nickel might appear as "VDI = 18 Nickel" on the display, or "VDI = 80 Dime, Penny."

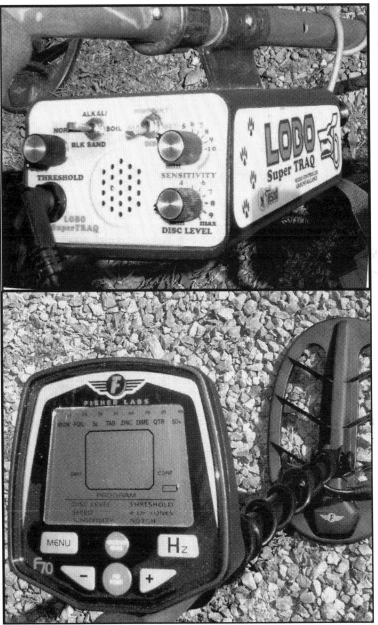

Figure 10. The Tesoro Lobo Super TRAQ uses tones for Target ID (top). The Fisher Labs F70 uses an LCD display with 2-digit VDI numbers (bottom).

Target Identification is not always accurate. The error rate tends to go up when the target is deeper in the ground.

3. Sensitivity

Sensitivity refers to the ability to detect metal objects from a distance. It is something akin to the volume control knob on an amplifier. Set too low, you won't hear the music. Set too high and you get distortion and chatter. Most detectors with sensitivity control have a mark on the control panel where the manufacturer recommends you set the dial. Under certain conditions, such as areas of high mineral content, or near power lines, it may be necessary to lower the sensitivity to cut down on noises and false signals.

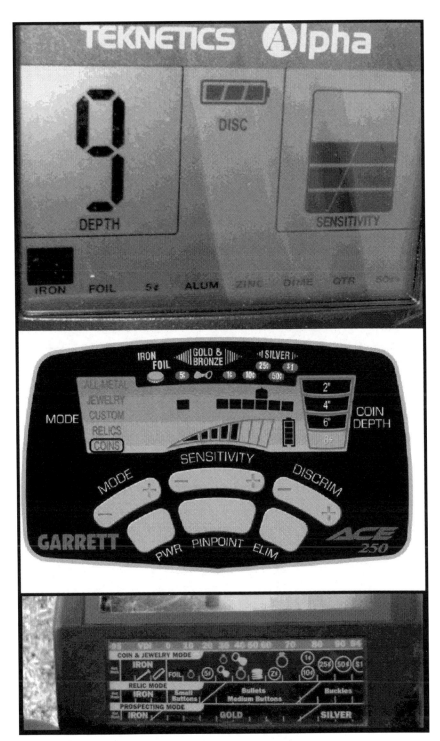

Figure 11. The discrimination display in some detectors is divided into broad categories. The Teknetics Alpha, top, has 8 categories: Iron, Foil, 5-cents, etc. The Garrett Ace 250, center, has 12: some are grayed-out in the photo. The White's MXT, bottom, uses VDI numbers ranging from -95 to +95, providing a much greater level of detail than the categories. This improved resolution makes the detector more expensive.

"How deep can I go with this coil?" The truth is, nobody can really say how deep a coil goes, due to the variables mentioned above. To be on the safe side, consider the half and half idea: You can easily find coins down to a depth of half your coil diameter. If you're using an 8-inch circular coil, you'll typically find coins at 4 inches. Your skill and patience pays off with the next 4 inches. Under ideal circumstances – good ground conditions, finely tuned detector, experienced operator, a flat-lying silver coin, and fresh batteries – you might gain another 4 inches on that same coil. This of course is just a general observation. There are experts in this hobby who will swear they can find coins much deeper than 8 inches using an 8-inch coil.

4. Search depth

The depth that your machine is able to search for coins depends on a number of factors. These include:

- Detector operating frequency. The lower frequencies have better depth.
- The strength of the magnetic field created by the detector; the stronger the field, the deeper the penetration.
- The size and shape of the search coil. Generally the larger the coil, the deeper it can search. Some coils employ two separate D-shaped windings. These "DD" coils distort the shape of the magnetic field and enable deeper searching.
- The composition of the ground being searched and its electrical characteristics. This is usually referred to simply as "mineralization", but it may include such variables as how tightly the ground is compacted, the presence of water, and the chemical makeup of the soil.
- The shape, size, and orientation of the object. A dime buried on its edge, for example, would be more difficult to detect than one laying flat (parallel to the surface).

5. Ground balance

All soils contain some degree of metals, such as iron, which can interfere with a detector's ability to find coins. **Ground Balance** allows the detector to see past these minerals. There are different ways to set ground balance:

- **Factory preset** ground balance. Here the manufacturer sets the ground balance at a predetermined level, which they estimate will work adequately in most searching environments. This "fixed" ground balance may be a less desirable compromise, but it lowers costs and works well in normal soil conditions.

- **Automatic** ground balance. Many modern detectors now employ circuitry which detects and adjusts for ground effects automatically.
- **Manual** ground balance. Manual ground balance requires the user to adjust for ground balance at the start of each searching session. This is a simple procedure where the user adjusts a setting on the detector with the coil alternately up in the air, then near the ground. Some detectorists prefer manual ground balance, at least as an option, since it provides greater control in prospecting, where changes in ground conditions are important for assessing the presence of gold-bearing ore.
- **Mixed** or combined methods of ground balance. Manufacturers often allow owners to select manual or automatic ground balancing, simply by flipping a toggle switch on the detector. As mentioned above, in some circumstances, such as prospecting for gold, the owner may want more control over settings on the detector. Think of it as automatic transmission versus a manual clutch.

6. Detector operating frequency

Detectors use very low frequency sine wave oscillations in the coil to detect their targets. The vast majority of detectors on the market today use an operating frequency between 3,000 and 20,000 cycles per second, or Hertz. The typical land-oriented detector might use an oscillator at 7,000 cycles per second, abbreviated 7 kHz.

For purposes of selecting a detector, the crucial point to remember is:

- The higher the frequency, the easier it is to detect small objects, such as BB-sized relics or minute specs of gold. Higher frequencies, however, are less able to penetrate deep into the ground.

- The lower the frequency, the deeper your detector can scan, with the same sized coil. Lower frequencies, however, are less efficient at picking up very small objects.

Detector operating frequency is not like a computer clock speed, where the faster it goes the better. The different frequencies are more suited for specific purposes. For high frequencies, imagine shooting sewing needles into the sand. They are good for picking up tiny objects, but they don't go very deep beneath the surface. Next shoot hundreds of nails into the sand. They go deeper than the needles, and are good for detecting coin-sized objects. Finally, shoot a few large tent stakes into the sand. They penetrate much deeper, but are not good at finding tiny objects. They are suited for finding larger objects.

Some manufacturers now produce detectors which generate multiple simultaneous frequencies for the same coil. This type of detector will span a much greater spectrum of both depth and object size. The Minelab Safari metal detector, for example, boasts 28 frequencies. Although this improves your detecting options, it also adds to the cost of the detector.

G. Examples of detector discrimination

The best way to understand the discrimination function on different detectors is to look at some examples. Familiarity with these three varieties of discrimination will help you make an informed decision regarding the trade-offs between the price of the detector and its' performance in the field. The following are typical examples, chosen for illustration purposes only.

It helps to think of the quality of discriminations as akin to pixels on a camera. A 1-megapixel camera will take a low resolution photo, while a 16-megapixel will cost more but will produce much higher quality photos.

1. Tesoro Silver Umax

The Tesoro Silver Umax is an excellent machine with good discrimination capabilities, and its light weight makes it a breeze to use for long periods. This detector uses sounds to indicate the type of target you have detected. The control box is shown below. Notice that there is a speaker but no LCD display or meter. The audio tone is broken and clipped when you scan junk, but produces a solid, repeatable signal for coins. See Figure 12.

There are just three controls. At the bottom left is the mode switch. For coin hunting, you would set the toggle switch to the center position, into Discrimination mode. This activates the dial above it, the Discrimination control. It may be a little hard to see in the photo, but if you set the Discrimination dial to the 12 O'clock position (5-cents), you will be able to detect nickels and everything above that setting, including pull-tabs (1 O'clock position), dimes and quarters. Similarly, foil (10 O'clock) and iron (9 O'clock) will be "discriminated out" and not produce a signal. This adjustment of the discrimination dial, and what it means, is the only real learning curve for this machine, but once you master the sounds and get to know the meaning of discrimination, you will have excellent detecting results.

• There are ways to fine tune this setting to effectively notch out the junk pull-tab signals. For example, with the Discrimination set to 5-cents you may get a signal. Then you move discrimination dial to the Tab position and you still get the same response. That's most likely a pull-tab. On the other hand, if you get a signal at the 5-cents position, but it goes away when you move the Discrimination dial up to the Tab position, this means you have blocked out a nickel signal. The experienced user will also be able to make out differences in the smoothness and amplitude of the sound which helps distinguish a nickel from a pull-tab even without touching the discrimination setting. Adjusting the Discrimination dial then allows you to tell the difference between a nickel and a pull tab. You can use the same

41

technique to distinguish between a pull-tab and a dime, or quarter, and so forth.

The Sensitivity dial is usually set when you first start detecting, and it's positioned so you get the loudest possible signal without chatter or static. This is usually around the 7 or 8 on the dial, and it will generally work well unless your ground conditions change. Most detectorists will use a set of head-phones while detecting. This is both a courtesy to other people and saves on battery power.

Figure 12. Control panel dials on the Tesoro Silver Umax. Adjusting the discrimination dial, left, helps you distinguish between coins and junk.

2. Garrett Ace 250

The Garrett Ace 250 adds a display to the discrimination function, as well as the ability to "notch out" undesirable portions of the dial. As you can see in the illustration below, there are 12 discrimination "segments" in the upper middle portion of the display. The instrument is set to the Coins mode, so some of the segments are grayed-out. These are the lower ranges of the discrimination spectrum; iron, foil and bottle caps. The grayed-out blocks mean that you won't hear a signal for those objects.

Notice too that the area of the spectrum above nickels but lower than pennies is also grayed out. This means you will not be bothered by all those beeps from pull-tabs. You can imagine that such a setting is pretty handy for finding coins. The only drawback is that some jewelry and gold rings fall into the same slots as the pull-tabs, so by notching out those segments you may be missing valuable finds. You can see the words "Gold & Bronze" in the same area as the pull-tab icon on the upper part of the display. See Figure 13.

When you set the mode to Jewelry, these segments become active once again, and you will hear a beep for both gold rings and pull-tabs. In the All-Metal mode, all the segments are lit up and active. In Custom mode you can pick which segments to enable. This ability to pick and choose which segments of the discrimination spectrum you want to activate adds a tremendous amount of flexibility and customizability to your metal detecting.

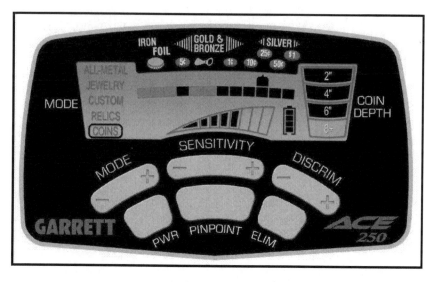

Figure 13. Control panel on the Garret Ace 250. In Coins mode, iron and foil are "notched out," as well as the pull-tabs between 5-cents and a penny, as shown by the grayed-out notches.

In the photograph of the Ace 250 display you can see a chevron type pointer above the segment for a 25-cent coin. This pointer changes position based on the type of object found by the coil. Many Ace 250 owners prefer to work in All-Metal mode then use both the chevron indicator and the quality of the sound in the headphones to determine whether or not to dig the target. For example, the user might get a signal for segment 6, the portion for a pull-tab just below the penny zone, and then choose not to dig it.

From experience you learn that pull-tabs often create a short, clipped, chirping signal and they may sound different when scanned in the East-West direction versus the North-South direction (because they are not symmetrical) whereas a ring has more of a steady, solid, repeatable sound, and it produces the same response no matter which direction you scan it from. Such a signal is a good prospect to dig.

3. White's MXT All Pro detector

The more expensive White's MXT takes the discrimination function to a higher level. Instead of just 12 zones or segments as found in the Ace 250, the MXT, like many advanced detectors, uses Visual Display Indication (VDI) numbers that are very specific in identifying a target. This enables much more acute discrimination between junk and valuable objects. After a while, the user begins to memorize different numbers and what type of target is associated with each. A nickel for example might register as a VDI value of 18 on the display, while a pull-tab will register as a 23. You would dig a target at 18, but not one at 23. Likewise, a 79 or 80 is usually a dime, and an 81 is a silver dime. That level of resolution, the ability to discriminate between similar objects, makes the VDI type of discrimination display the gold standard among detectors.

With the VDI type of detector, you learn very quickly what values represent which coins, and whether they are clad or silver coins too. You also learn common VDI numbers for pull-tabs, and this saves you a lot of digging time. VDI numbers for rings and jewelry often range all across the spectrum, due to differences in their shape, metallic composition (gold, silver, etc.), and weight. Figure 14 shows a VDI display.

Figure 14. VDI display of a White's detector. VDI numbers are specific and repeatable for common coins, which provides the operator much more resolution than the broad categories of less expensive machines.

4. A tool is just a tool

Remember, the discrimination function is just a tool. A curious thing happens once you become experienced in using such technology. In time, you begin to learn to identify targets from sound alone. You can focus in on the quality of the sound (clipped, broken, symmetrical increase and decrease, amplitude, etc.), its repeatability when scanned from different directions, and its properties when you switch to pin-pointer mode. Once you've learned the sounds, you don't have to rely on the discrimination display as much as you did when first starting out. After listening to thousands of signals, you can pretty much guess, with a good level of accuracy, the only decision that's important: whether to dig the signal or not. People who have achieved that level of expertise will sometimes then choose to go back to a lighter, simpler detector, such as one with no VDI display.

4. The Art of Choosing a Detector

A. Detector choices

As mentioned earlier, the essential strategy in selecting a detector is as follows.

1. Understand the concepts of Discrimination and Target ID in order to evaluate which detector is best for you. This was covered in the previous chapter, in particular Section G, Examples of Discrimination, page 40.

2. Know which types of metal detecting are available in your area. For the beginner, this is not a problem because you will want to start with a general purpose detector, not a costly water or gold detector. A general purpose metal detector will certainly let you know if you come across a gold nugget. Most detectors also have submersible coils, so you can stick the business end into the water if necessary.

3. Finally, consider your budget and activity level. You don't want to spend a small fortune on a detector just to see it collect dust in your garage.

The next section will help determine your goals and budget, item 3, above. Let's compare some popular models at various price ranges.

B. Price categories

If you are just curious about metal detecting, don't want to spend very much, or just want something for children to play with, then a detector in the $100 price range may be an option for you.

You will find coins even with inexpensive detectors. These can work well for beginners but such machines are generally considered poor in discrimination ability and durability. If your budget cannot go above $100 or so, you may want to consider a used model that has better quality discrimination.

The more serious hobbyist choice for a new detector will start around $200. In the $200 to $300 price range you start to get good quality discrimination and rugged design for longer hours of detecting.

As you become more expert, you will appreciate the value of quality discrimination ability. The mid-range detectors will have a two-digit Target ID display, or Visual Discrimination Indicator (VDI), that is quite specific in identifying what's in the ground.

With these considerations in mind, let's take a look at detectors in different price categories. The following charts will help you choose a first detector. Not all models are shown here. Rather, the more popular models with a good number of reviews are included. Newer models, such as the Minelab Go-Find series, do not have a long enough history to evaluate in these charts.

NOTE: Ratings in the charts are relative. A user who spends $100 for a detector and finds 100 coins might be just as happy with his purchase as someone who spends $700 and finds 300 coins in the same amount of time. Ratings and number of reviews are composite scores from multiple sources. The rating is a rough estimate of value, and the number of reviews is a rough estimate of popularity.

C. Under $200 price category

These are the low-end detector models. The new Minelab models, Go-Find 20 and Go-Find 40 are in this group but there are too few reviews available for reliable rankings.

Rank by user ratings: under $200.

Rank by User Rating			
Under $200		Ratings	
Price	Brand	Model	Rank
$160	Tesoro	Compadre	1
$195	Bounty Hunter	Discovery 3300	2
$110	Bounty Hunter	Discovery 1100	3
$172	Bounty Hunter	Timeranger	4
$190	Bounty Hunter	Quickdraw II	5
$90	Bounty Hunter	Tracker IV	6
$155	Garrett	Ace 150	7
$54	Bounty Hunter	GoldDigger	8
$170	Bounty Hunter	Sharpshooter II	9
$180	White's	Coinmaster	10
$133	Bounty Hunter	Quicksilver	11
$41	Bounty Hunter	Junior BHJS	12

Note: The new Minelab Go-Find 20 & 40 are in this group, but there are too few reviews to establish ratings.

Table 1. Rank by user rating in the under $200 category.

Rank by number of reviews; a rough estimate of popularity: under $200.

Rank by Number of Reviews			
Under $200		Number Reviews	
Price	Brand	Model	Rank
$54	Bounty Hunter	GoldDigger	1
$41	Bounty Hunter	Junior BHJS	2
$90	Bounty Hunter	Tracker IV	3
$133	Bounty Hunter	Quicksilver	4
$155	Garrett	Ace 150	5
$170	Bounty Hunter	Sharpshooter II	6
$172	Bounty Hunter	Timeranger	7
$195	Bounty Hunter	Discovery 3300	8
$118	Bounty Hunter	Lonestar	9
$160	Tesoro	Compadre	10
$110	Bounty Hunter	Discovery 1100	11
$190	Bounty Hunter	Quickdraw II	12

Note: The new Minelab Go-Find 20 & 40 are in this group, but there are too few reviews to establish ratings.

Table 2. Rank by number of reviews in the under $200 category.

D. $200 to $399 price category

Rank by user ratings: $200 to $399. The new Minelab models, Go-Find 60 is in this group but there are too few reviews available for reliable rankings.

Rank by User Rating			
$200 - $399		**Ratings**	
Price	**Brand**	**Model**	**Rank**
$260	Tesoro	Silver uMax	1
$220	Teknetics	EuroTek Pro	2
$250	Teknetics	Delta 4000	3
$365	Tesoro	Cibola	4
$300	Garrett	Ace 350	5
$210	Bounty Hunter	Pioneer 202	6
$300	Minelab	Xterra 305*	7
$212	Garrett	Ace 250	8
$215	Fisher	F-2	9
$293	Bounty Hunter	Landstar	10
$280	White's	Coinmaster Pro	11
$300	Bounty Hunter	Pioneer 505	12

* Discontinued, but still available.

Table 3. Rank by user rating in the $200 to $399 category.

Rank by number of reviews; a rough estimate of popularity: $200 to $399.

Rank by Number of Reviews			
$200 - $399		**Number Reviews**	
Price	Brand	Model	Rank
$212	Garrett	Ace 250	1
$215	Fisher	F-2	2
$365	Tesoro	Cibola	3
$260	Tesoro	Silver uMax	4
$300	Garrett	Ace 350	5
$300	Bounty Hunter	Pioneer 505	6
$250	Teknetics	Delta 4000	7
$210	Bounty Hunter	Pioneer 202	8
$293	Bounty Hunter	Landstar	9
$280	White's	Coinmaster Pro	10
$220	Teknetics	EuroTek Pro	11
$300	Minelab	Xterra 305*	12

* Discontinued, but still available.

Table 4. Rank by number of reviews in the $200 to $399 category.

E. $400 to $799 price category

Rank by user ratings: $400 to $799.

Rank by User Rating			
$400 - $799		**Ratings**	
Price	**Brand**	**Model**	**Rank**
$555	Tesoro	Outlaw	1
$640	White's	Matrix M6	2
$680	Tesoro	Lobo SuperTRAQ (G)	3
$450	Tesoro	Vaquero	4
$505	Fisher	F5	5
$600	Tesoro	Tejon	6
$665	Fisher	F70	7
$765	Fisher	Gold Bug 2 (G)	8
$510	Tesoro	DeLeon	9
$580	Tesoro	Sand Shark (W)	10
$680	Garrett	AT Gold (G)	11
$725	Tesoro	Cortes	12

Table 5. Rank by user rating in the $400 to $799 category.
(G) = Gold; (W) = Water.

Rank by number of reviews; a rough estimate of popularity: $400 to $799.

Rank by Number of Reviews			
$400 - $799		**Number Reviews**	
Price	**Brand**	**Model**	**Rank**
$600	Garrett	AT Pro (W)	1
$450	Tesoro	Vaquero	2
$640	White's	Matrix M6	3
$430	Fisher	F4	4
$600	Tesoro	Tejon	5
$680	Garrett	AT Gold (G)	6
$505	Fisher	F5	7
$765	Fisher	Gold Bug 2 (G)	8
$665	Fisher	F70	9
$680	Tesoro	Lobo SuperTRAQ (G)	10
$580	Tesoro	Sand Shark (W)	11
$725	Tesoro	Cortes	12

Table 6. Rank by number of reviews in the $400 to $799 category. (G) = Gold; (W) = Water.

F. $800 and over price category

Rank by user ratings: $800 or more.

Rank by User Rating			
$800 or more		**Ratings**	
Price	Brand	Model	Rank
$1,115	Minelab	Safari	1
$1,100	White's	Spectra Vx3	2
$800	White's	MXT Tracker	3
$825	White's	Surf PI (W)	4
$810	Fisher	CZ 3D	5
$825	White's	MXT All Pro	6
$900	Teknetics	T2	7
$1,200	Minelab	Explorer SE	8
$1,065	Garrett	Infinium LS (W)	9
$935	Garrett	GTI 2500	10
$950	Fisher	F75	11
$1,200	Minelab	Excalibur 1000 (W)	12

Table 7. Rank by user rating in the $800 and over category.
(G) = Gold; (W) = Water.

Rank by number of reviews; a rough estimate of popularity: $800 or more.

Rank by Number of Reviews			
$800 or more		**Number Reviews**	
Price	**Brand**	**Model**	**Rank**
$800	White's	MXT Tracker	1
$935	Garrett	GTI 2500	2
$950	Fisher	F75	3
$1,200	Minelab	Excalibur 1000 (W)	4
$810	Fisher	CZ 3D	5
$900	Teknetics	T2	6
$1,065	Garrett	Infinium LS (W)	7
$1,000	Minelab	Eureka Gold (G)	8
$1,115	Minelab	Safari	9
$1,200	Minelab	Explorer SE	10
$1,100	White's	Spectra Vx3	11
$915	White's	BeachHunter 300 (W)	12

Table 8. Rank by number of reviews in the $800 and over category. (G) = Gold; (W) = Water.

G. Suggestions Along the Way

First Suggestion: Buy a new general purpose detector.

New detectors often come with a warranty, so you know they will work out of the box. The specialty detectors for water and prospecting cost much more and you shouldn't need that level of specialization as a first detector. If you are new to the hobby, buy from a brick-and-mortar store as opposed to online. Prices remain competitive and you will get extras and personal care that is priceless.

Second Suggestion: Find a helper.

Metal detecting is quite a popular hobby, and you may already know some people in the game. If at all possible, arrange to go on a short hunt with someone who owns a detector. Most are more than happy to demonstrate how the system works. Many detector clubs exist that have programs to guide new users.

Third Suggestion: Stay within your budget.

Don't go hog wild and overspend on your first detector. Take baby steps. If you really need to upgrade at a later point you can always sell the lower-grade detector and move up. That is a much safer strategy than spending good money on a top-of-the-line detector only to find it is not a match for your needs.

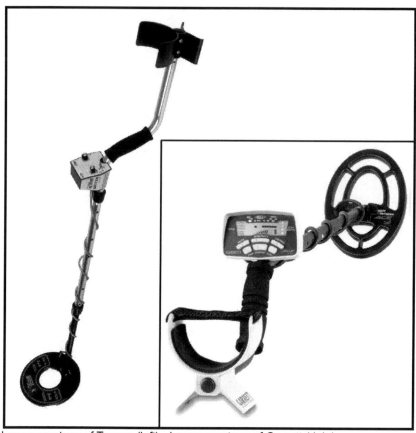
Image courtesy of Tesoro (left). Image courtesy of Garrett (right)

Figure 15. Two affordable metal detectors: The Tesoro Silver Umax (left), and the Garrett Ace 250 (right).

Fourth Suggestion: Make a Check List

Using the criteria above, plot out what's important to you. For review, your checklist should include at least the following:

- **Discrimination / Target ID.** This is important. A low cost detector might be able to tell the difference between a nail and a nickel, but not between a pull-tab and a nickel, which are close to each other on the discrimination scale. A high-end detector will be able to tell the difference between a copper penny (prior to 1982) and a clad penny (copper-coated zinc penny). How much are you willing to spend to have more precise Target ID?
- **Sensitivity.** This comes down to a dial or setting that adjusts sensitivity. Set too low, you will miss many targets. Set too high, you may have a high noise level.
- **Depth.** This is a hard one to gauge. Normally the larger the coil diameter the deeper you can find things, but detector circuit design is also a powerful factor.
- **Ground balance.** Many detectors have fixed ground balance, which works well in most soils. If you plan to work in areas with high salt content or alkaline deposits, adjusting ground balance may be important.
- **Operating Frequency.** Detector engineers will generally make the best choice in operating frequency for any particular detector, so you shouldn't have to worry too much over this. Lower frequencies may penetrate deeper into the ground, while higher frequencies are better at finding the smallest items. This may be a factor in gold prospecting, but not so much in coin detecting. Some high-end detectors have multiple or adjustable operating frequencies.
- **Weight.** The weight of the detector affects how long you can comfortably swing the device. From the online forums, weight seems to be a big issue.
- **Batteries.** The batteries add weight to the detector, but more power means you don't have to switch out the batteries as often.

Figure 16. Two other popular choices: the White's M6, top, and the Garrett AT Pro, bottom.

H. Checklist for models around $200

Let's look at three popular models in the $200 range. These are all from leading manufacturers and have good reviews. Here we compare their specifications. Add more categories, such as adjustable ground balance, if necessary for your personal wishes.

	Minelab Go-Find 60	Garrett Ace 250	Fisher F-2
Street Price	$270	$210	$215
Batteries	AA x4	AA x4	9-v x2
Discrim. & Target ID	4 icon segments & tones	12 icon segments & 3 tones	8 segments, 4 tones, 95 VDI numbers
Adjust Sens.	Yes	Yes	Yes
Coil Size (depth)	10 inch	6.5x9 inch	8 inch
Coil Change	No	Yes	Yes
Op. Freq.	7.7 kHz	6.5 kHz	5.9 kHz
Weight	2.3 lbs.	2.7 lbs.	2.6 lbs.
Comments	New model; collapsible; phone app.	Best-seller, good reviews; good TID	Notch Discrim.; TID numbers a big plus.

Table 9. Comparison of detector models around $200.

With the chart filled in from the checklist, you're in a much better position to evaluate the three models. In summary, they all come in at a decent price, and all of them have dials for discrimination and sensitivity. One disappointment is that they all have fixed ground balance.

The Minelab Go-Find 60 is relatively new and doesn't have many reviews. It is, however, from a respected manufacturer with a history of quality designs. It has the largest coil and folds up for easy travel.

The Garrett Ace 250 is by far the most popular model for serious metal detecting. It is recommended for beginners. Owners give it good reviews. The 12 segment Target Identification is not as good as the 2-digit codes that you get with more advanced machines, but it is enough to distinguish various types of targets.

The Fisher Labs F2 is budget friendly and has an 8-inch coil. The big plus here is the 2-digit Target Identification number that you find on higher-priced models. This adds a lot to the ability to discriminate trash from treasure.

Although easy-to-use discrimination displays are essential to beginning metal detecting enthusiasts, it's not the only factor in choosing a detector. Many detectorists dig up everything that produces a signal, such as in relic hunting. Others have the ability to assess target value from the sound of the signal alone. For these people, Target ID is not so important. In such cases a simple, effective detector is all you need. The Tesoro Silver Umax, for example, is a popular model that gets high ratings. Its street price is under $250. You can tune the discrimination dial to identify targets, but often you don't need to fiddle with anything – you just dig it up and see what you find. It is light weight, 2.2 pounds, so it's easy on the arms on a long hunt.

Again, these comments are not meant as an iron-clad review of the value of any of the detectors. The idea here is to make a chart up for yourself, listing what is important to you, so you can make your own comparisons and choose the best combination of features for yourself. You might decide, for example, that you get more bang for your buck by purchasing a used detector. Perhaps you want to consider a different price range.

I. Checklist for $600 models

Next we look at some higher priced detectors. After you've been detecting for a while you may get a hankering for some of the advanced features available on the more expensive machines.

As suggested above, *Suggestions Along the Way*, page 57, it helps to compare notes with other detectorists. When I first got started in detecting I joined a club, and we would spread out our finds on the ground after each hunt. I was using a Garrett Ace 250 at the time. I was quite happy with the machine and how effective it was, but club members with more advanced models would consistently find more coins and at greater depths. I was detecting at least twice a week, so I felt it was worthwhile to spend the extra money for a more capable detector.

Use the price-category table listings to select some candidates for consideration. Most people buy the higher cost models only after they are familiar with what the improved capabilities can offer them. Again, it is suggested you make up a comparison chart for the models you are considering. Some detector manufacturer web sites, and some distributors such as KellyCo (http://www.kellycodetectors.com/) have online applications that allow you to compare model specifications side by side.

These three models were selected for comparison purposes. All of them are popular models with good ratings.

	Fisher F5, D-D coil	Garrett AT Pro	White's Matrix M6
Street Price	$550	$600	$640
Batteries	9-v x2	AA x4	AA x8
Discrim. & Target ID	99 TID #s, 8 segments, 4 tone IDs	99 TID #s 12 notch seg., 3 tone IDs	190 VDI numbers, 7 tone IDs
Adjust Sens.	Yes	Yes	Yes
Coil Size (depth)	11" D-D coil	8.5 x 11" D-D	9.5" round
Coil Change	Yes	Yes	Yes
Op. Freq.	7.8 kHz	15 kHz	14 kHz
Weight	2.9	3.3	4.0
Ground Bal.	Manual	Auto & Manual	Auto & Manual
Search Modes	3	6	3
Comments	Frequency shift	Waterproof to 10 feet; target conductivity	Good depth, beach reviews;

Table 10. More advanced detector models.

All three models have two-digit Target ID numbers, or VDI codes, for improved discrimination. The Fisher F5 is a light-weight model that comes with the optional 11-inch D-D coil. Round coils have a bowl-shaped search field, while the D-D coils have a flatter field, closer to a pancake shape. This improves the depth and pinpointing abilities. The White's model comes with a round coil but has a D-D option at additional cost.

The Garret AT Pro is a best-seller in that price range. It is also waterproof to 10-foot depth for beach and lake use. The White's is also quite popular and has excellent discrimination abilities.

4. A used detector

Buying a used detector can add to the quality of the features you get for the money. Just be sure everything is working properly. Don't buy a detector that is very old as you may be getting a dinosaur. The detector should at least have decent discrimination capabilities. A used machine may have better functionality, but there is always the risk of something breaking or wearing out. If you are unsure about evaluating a used detector then this is a motivation to buy a new one.

> "Modern computerized circuitry will find more treasure and will find it quicker and easier than even the best of yesterday's instruments."
> - Charles Garrett, *How to Find Lost Treasure*

If you are buying a used detector:
- You can generally find the user manual by going to the web site of the manufacturer.
- Check the battery case for corrosion, and clean it if necessary. Put in fresh batteries.
- Check the cable from the control box to the coil. Look for frayed wires or nicks that might compromise the water-resistant properties of the coil.
- Adjust the shaft and arm rest to fit your height.
- Run an air test, or above ground test with different coins and see how the detector responds.
- As above, check the operation of the discriminator, the sensitivity dial, pin-pointer, and the depth reading. Investigate what other functions are featured for your detector.
- Read the manual!

Figure 17. A used detector might provide more features and adjustments for the same price. The well-respected Minelab X-Terra series is being phased out, but you can still find used and even new models for sale.

5. Related Detecting Equipment

A. Detector coils

Detectors come with a standard coil, usually between 6 and 10 inches around. After detecting for a while, you become familiar with ground conditions in your area. Trash-filled areas are easier to work with a smaller coil, which can separate responses from nearby targets. This makes it easier to find coins right next to junk. Smaller coils do not penetrate the ground as deeply as larger coils.

Oversized coils will penetrate deeper into the soil, but they are not as good at separating out two nearby targets. They are also heavier, and may create fatigue sooner than the lighter, smaller coils.

Many manufactures have models that allow you to attach coils of different sizes and shapes to your stock detector, in order to allow for junk-filled areas, greater depth, or a different field pattern. The smaller coils are great for hunting in trash-filled areas where you want the ability to separate out different signals. The larger coils are better for depth. The back-to-back D-shaped coils, usually called Double-D or D-D coils, distort the shape of the search field from a cone shape into something more like the blade of a shovel. See **Figure 18,** below.

This flat shape to the detection field makes it broader in one direction, so that swinging the detector from left to right and back again covers a lot more ground area than the cone shape. Larger coils for the same detector are often advertised for the greater depth they can reach. Choosing a larger coil must be considered along with the extra weight that comes with it. Depending on your strength and stamina, you might be able to swing a smaller, lighter coil for a longer period of time. Even with the extra weight, it's often to your advantage to get the extra depth for areas where deeply buried coins are in abundance.

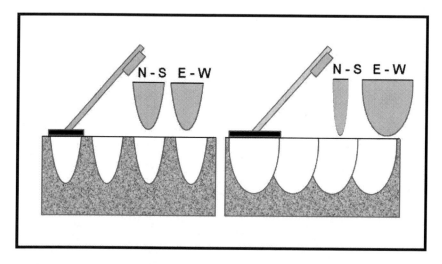

Figure 18. Side view of search area shows less coverage for a standard circular coil (left) versus a Double-D coil (right), for the same swing pattern. The field cross-section is narrow in the North-South direction for the D-D coil but broader in the East-West direction.

B. Hand-held pin-pointers

Most modern metal detectors have a pin-point function built into the circuitry, so all you have to do is press a button and you can zero in on the target. Technically then, you don't really need a separate hand-held pin-pointer. Once you work with one, however, you will see how much faster it's possible to retrieve a coin. Many coins turn a reddish brown color after being in the ground for decades, making it difficult to sift through the dirt for the coin. The pin-pointer makes fast work of that task.

There are different methods of pinpointing your target. You can use the built-in pin-pointer that is integral to your detector; you can buy a hand-held probe, or you can consider buying an **in-line probe** for your detector, Figure 19. An in-line probe is one specifically manufactured for your model of detector, and it is inserted by screw-in cables between your coil and the detector control box. The advantage is you can retain the depth and target ID readings on your machine as you search for the target with the smaller probe. This is especially helpful when you are in a trash-filled area and the hole you've dug has more than one metal object in it. One of the more popular manufacturers is Sun-Ray at http://www.sunraydetector.com/.

C. Detector attachments

Consider a **coil cover** to prevent scratches and scuffs on your coil. They only cost a few dollars each, and they keep your coil in a like-new condition.

If you detect in heavy grass or shrubbery, you'll notice the coil has a tendency to flop around, changing the angle it makes with the shaft. There is, after all, just a small plastic screw holding it in place. You can purchase a much stronger coil retaining device from most detector stores. This bracket holds the coil steady; it costs only a few dollars.

(Example:
http://www.kellycodetectors.com/accessories/lejermonharnesses.
htm.)

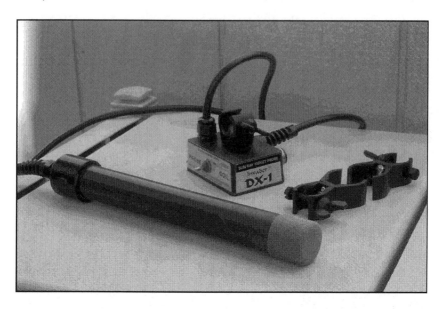

Figure 19. An in-line probe connects directly to your control box and
extends the detectors discrimination abilities to the hand-held device.

Rain covers are available for many detectors. You want to have
protection from unexpected rain. Detectors can be damaged if
water gets into the electronics. Sometimes you can find a clear
plastic bag or zip-lock bag that will work in a pinch. Several
stores also offer shoulder or hip harnesses that help bear the
weight of the detector. These strap-on devices relieve some of the
weight from your arm and transfer it to your body frame.
(Example:
http://www.kellycodetectors.com/accessories/lejermonharnesses.
htm.)

A decent pair of **headphones** is a must. Headphones will save
your batteries, and cut down on the annoyance factor for people
around you. Don't try to get by with the cheap ear-buds that
come with your telephone or music player. They will fall out

way too often, and the thin wires are simply not up to the task of rugged activity.

D. Digging tools and probes

You will definitely need some method of digging up the coins. There are narrow probes, like an ice pick, that can help locate the coin. The digging tool itself can vary in size and length depending on ground conditions. For some locations, you might need a simple flat-head screwdriver, and for others a narrow hand-held spade or scoop. For deeper coins, a larger digging tool is required. Sometimes a sod plug tool is handy for retrieving coins while preserving the appearance of the lawn.

You can buy simple gardening supplies to fill the task, though there are quite a few handy tools made specifically for metal detector digging, Figure 20. This includes the trowel with inch marks to show how deep you are, and a saw-tooth edge for cutting roots.

Decide if a mechanical probe, like an ice pick, is right for you. Some locations have too many rocks for this to be effective, but if you live in an area that is mostly rock-free clay or sandy soil, using a pick to locate the coin will save you time, and it's less of a mess than digging a hole.

Lesche brand **digging tools** are ideal for metal detecting. They are available at most detector stores. If you want a less expensive version, go to the gardening department of the hardware store. They have all sorts of serrated-edge trowels, diggers, weeders, and hand shovels - maybe not as dedicated to metal detecting, but they will do the job.

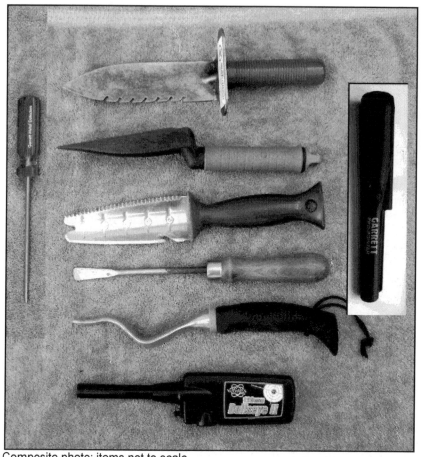

Composite photo: items not to scale.

Figure 20. Digging tools and probes make retrieving your finds easier.

E. Protective gear and conveniences

Bring an old **tool belt** or fabric apron that has at least three pockets. Again, you can find good ones at the thrift store. Many detecting buffs like to sort their finds while in the field. Keep coins in one pocket, junk in another, and probes in the third.

Do your arms get tired after detecting for a while? Consider purchasing a strap to transfer the weight of the detector from your arm to a shoulder or belt harness. The major detector distributors sell both shoulder and belt harnesses at reasonable prices.

Knee pads really help for detecting. They make it easier and more comfortable to kneel down; they keep your pants cleaner, and they are a must-have item for wet ground.

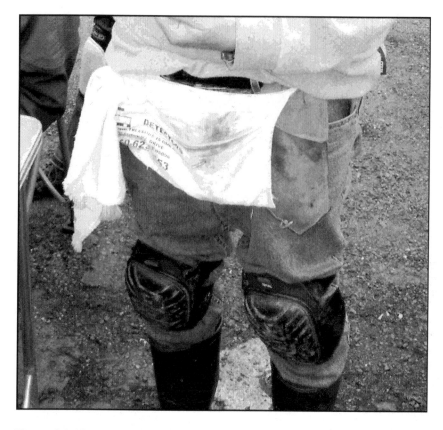

Figure 21. Knee pads and a towel come in handy.

You can find knee pads real cheap at almost any thrift store, especially after soccer season is over. Use a **towel** or a small plastic drop cloth when digging holes. Once you've cut the plug and you start scooping out the dirt, pour the loose dirt on the towel. It makes finding the coin much easier, and allows you to funnel the dirt back in the hole when you're done. That leaves cleaner grass and a less noticeable plug in the ground.

The towel is useful, too, for spreading out and counting your coins and finds at the end of the day.

Many detectorists carry a small **water bottle** filled half way with soapy water. They drop their coins in them, which then slosh around as they hunt. This is often all the cleaning they will need, so that when you get home, you just dry them off and sort them out. Likewise, many bring a water bottle for drinking. (Don't get them mixed up!)

Always carry some extra **plastic bags**. These are good for storing trash, carrying larger items that are covered in dirt or mud, and they are handy for keeping your detector dry, should it suddenly start to rain.

Bring an eye loupe, or small **magnifier**, to help you identify coins in the field. Some older coins have a lot of wear and you may need help reading the date.

Keep the following nearby; perhaps in your car:

- Buckets, boxes and bags (keep them in the car) just in case you find something big, dirty, or private that you want to cart back home
- Extra towels, water, soap, or disposable cleansing pads to clean up.
- Extra headphones
- Extra gloves
- Extra batteries
- A First-Aid Kit.

F. Clothing and safety

Think of your own safety and comfort while you are detecting.
Here are some tips:
- Always carry a cell phone so you can communicate if you get into trouble.
- Consider a whistle or pepper spray for protection
- Always carry a couple of band-aids.
- Never stick your fingers into a hole to feel around for the coin. It may be a sharp or jagged piece of metal, a knife, or other dangerous object.
- Wear long pants and a good set of boots, especially if you are in territory with ticks, snakes, briars, or barbed wire.
- Don't go out in a lightning storm.

"There are three things you can do to mitigate travel problems: drive a reliable vehicle, carry a vehicle safety kit, and maintain a positive attitude while traveling"
- *Safe Journeys*, Gray B. Speck, W&E Treasures magazine, June, 2003.

Finally, always protect yourself against stinging insects, such as fire ants, bees, and mosquitoes. You can do this with protective clothing and hats, as well as with insect repellent.

If you want to maintain domestic tranquility, you should consider having heavy-duty clothing reserved specifically for metal detecting, and you can keep it out in the garage. Let's face it: you are going to get dirty. Shoes are the biggest factor, as they can track in mud, and will get plenty of wear. Consider a rugged pair of high top boots. Do not buy steel-toed boots, as the metal will set off the detector every time your foot comes into range. Get a good pair of long-johns for cold weather.

Gloves are handy for protecting your skin and keeping your fingers clean.

6. The Art of the Hunt

A. General guidelines

<u>1. Go where people walk</u>

Probably the single most important decision you will make is where you decide to go searching. That choice will strongly influence what you find, and how much you will find. Search site planning will pay off in the long run with more valuable finds.

Rule of Thumb: Search where lots of people have walked.

Think about it. If you go out into some isolated forest, what will you find? Who is out there? Maybe a hunter or horseman passed that way long ago. Accordingly, you will find only an occasional shell casing, or perhaps a metal button or clasp. If you go to an elementary school site you're going to find pencils, pennies, and small metal toys. And if you go to a college campus, you're increasing your chances of finding more valuable coins, and more expensive jewelry. The key here is to find a site where many people congregated, and over a period of many years.

Figure 22. This unpaved footpath next to a busy street has seen a lot of human traffic.

2. Talk to the man (or woman)

People are nice. Don't be afraid of them. Sometimes, in order to search a site you will need to talk to the owner, the landlord, the facility manager, the groundskeeper, or a caretaker. If you are new to this, the first time you ask for permission to hunt on private property may be a little awkward, but it opens up a whole new vista of opportunity for you. When I first started, I was too shy to ask. There was a street I was working that had a median strip down the center, and I was detecting along the median. Several residents were curious. They were friendly enough to approach me and asked what I was finding. It was only one more step for me to summon up the courage to ask if I could search the strip in front of their house. From then on it was easy. It turned out the sections of grass between the house and the street are much more productive than the median strip. I showed my finds to the owners. They talked about getting their own detector! Just put a smile on your face, be brave, and ask for what you want. That approach is sure to open many doors for you.

Figure 23. A shady tree by a school is a good place to hunt.

B. Keep it legal

Be sure to check local regulations: many municipalities have restrictions about metal detecting at historic or environmentally sensitive public sites. Many detector clubs and their web sites will list local regulations.

Stay on the right side of the law. You should know about the **Archaeological Resources Protection Act of 1979.** Become familiar with the ARPA law: it requires a permit to remove anything from protected land.

> The purpose of this Act is to secure, for the present and future benefit of the American people, the protection of archaeological resources and sites which are on public lands and Indian lands, and to foster increased cooperation and exchange of information between governmental authorities, the professional archaeological community, and private individuals having collections of archaeological resources and data which were obtained before the date of the enactment of this Act.

And from the Bureau of Land Management (BLM):

- Metal detectors may be used for the noncommercial collection of nonrenewable resources such as rocks, mineral specimens, common invertebrates, fossils and semi-precious gemstones.

- The collection of minerals for sale or barter to commercial dealers may be done only after obtaining a contract or permit from an authorized officer of BLM.

- Metal detectors may not be used to collect any cultural or historic items which are protected by law.

- Items and structures such as historic old cabin sites or mining areas must not be disturbed, altered or impacted by the use of metal detectors. Digging under, alongside or above historic or archeological sites or resources is considered impacting to these resources and is prohibited by law.

- The collection of coins and bullets is allowed if these items are not found in a physical or proximity relationship with archaeological or historic resources.

C. If this is your first hunt

<u>1. The user manual</u>

If you're like most people, the minute you receive your detector, you'll put in the batteries and run out to the back yard to check it out. That's OK, but once the initial excitement dies down, the best thing you can do is to **READ THE MANUAL!** Every manufacturer, every treasure hunting expert, every online instruction, advises the same thing: read the user manual.

The manual will usually describe the factory recommended settings. These are generally marked as arrows or pointers on the dials. If you are getting a lot of chatter at those settings, you might have to turn down the "gain" or "sensitivity" dial.

Next, run an air test, or above ground test. Grab some coins, a bottle cap, and some other small metal objects, and bring them to an open area for testing. You will be surprised at the different sounds and meter readings you get with the various objects. Try playing with the discrimination control, and be sure you understand how that works before you go off into the field. Does your detector have Target Identification? How does that work on your air test of known targets?

<u>2. An easy search</u>

For your first outing, try a "tot lot." That is one of those parks for children that have wood chips or sand in a play area. The tot lot is easy to dig without causing damage, and it's often a good place to find a coin or two. Again, be sure to fiddle with the dials, especially the discriminator, to see what effects they have. When you first start, it's advisable to hunt in "All Metal Mode" which means you turn the discriminator down all the way. That means you will hear a tone for everything made of metal. Try the pin-pointer function. Check out the depth indicator. Oh, NOW do you see why you have to read the manual?!

Figure 24. A "Tot Lot" is a good place for beginners to hunt. The sand, wood chips or other mulch in these playgrounds is easy to dig and hides lots of treasures.

3. Around the house

If you're new to metal detecting, a good place to practice is around your own home. There are lots of places around the house where coins get lost, and this provides a convenient classroom for discovering all the possible places to search. There's an old wooden base supporting the water heater in my garage. I know that no daylight has penetrated behind or under that corner for decades. There's a two foot space between the old garage and the neighbor's fence. Do you suppose some coins could be out there?

Learn to explore all the nooks and crannies in your own back yard, and front yard too. It helps you think of unique places to search when you are away from home. Think of where most of the traffic is in your home. It may be the entrances, and the walkways on the side. This same type of analysis pays off when you search an abandoned homestead or a neighborhood school. It's strange that people spend most of their time indoors, yet little if any metal detecting is done inside buildings.

Modern building standards require that every hole and crevice be plugged against mice, insects and drafts, so people don't generally detect inside their homes. Throughout most of American history, however, these building standards were not so strict. Homes had creaky wooden floors and folks walked over to the outhouse to take care of business. If you live in a part of town where the houses were, or are, older than 100 years, then you know the ground is going to contain more coins than an area where a housing development went in just 10 years ago.

D. Using maps

<u>1. Current paper maps</u>

A city street map is probably the simplest and most direct method of finding a good place to hunt with your metal detector. Check the major thoroughfares and transit terminals. Look where people lived, worked and traveled. Where were the major population centers? Hotels? Boarding houses?

Once you have your city map, check out the following:
- Ball fields
- Beaches, lakes, riverbanks, swimming holes
- Bicycle trails
- Boat launches, marinas
- Campgrounds
- Fairgrounds
- Hiking trails
- Open space preserves
- Parks
- Picnic areas
- Recreation areas
- Schools
- Scout camps
- Sight-seeing points, vista viewpoints

Many maps include "Points of Interest" - check them out. Which ones have grassy areas or undeveloped land that would make for good detecting?

Many atlases and book-style maps, such as the Thomas Guide from Rand McNally, have indexes in the back which include all kinds of potential hunt sites. These include many on private property, so be sure to get permission first. Others are on private property, but the sidewalks, paths, and surrounding landscape is often on public land.

"Soft areas" refers to anything that you can dig, such as grass, sand, mulch, pine-needle areas, low-lying ground cover, gravel, pea-gravel, and plain old dirt. Oftentimes, around concrete, asphalt, and blacktop, you are unable to dig, but there are soft areas adjacent to even the most developed structures where you can find coins and treasures that have rolled away.

Be sure to include sites unique to your area, such as abandoned roads, horse trails, ranches, science centers, overlooks and vista points, gymnasiums, youth centers, animal parks, tennis clubs, theaters, tramways, art studios, racetracks, rodeo centers, visitor centers, conference halls, boardwalks, transportation terminals, cultural centers, and shopping malls. You get the idea. Maybe you can't hunt right ON the private property, but you can search along streets and grassy areas near these sites. The trick is to go where lots of people have walked or rested. You are responsible for knowing the laws that apply to your locale. Just looking at these points of interest, though, will generate some good search plans for your metal detecting.

> "So, if you're sincere about treasure hunting and want to be well prepared when you go out with your detector, take along a good map. At the very least, it will keep you from getting lost. At best, it may enable you to locate old sites which could yield real treasure."

> - Ed Chaffin, *Be Ready When You Go Afield*, *W&E Treasures* magazine, May, 1995.

In addition to street maps look for:

Transit maps showing bus routes, train stations, terminals, light-rail stations. These carry thousands of commuters and travelers. They often have to cross over parks, public land, vacant lots, trails, or promenades to gain access to the transportation. Many hotels and visitor bureaus hand out maps for points of interest in your town. Get one of those maps and see where people visit.

There are many **specialty maps** for particular audiences. Many can be found at your local library, tourist information sites, chambers of commerce, social groups, historic groups, and other special-interest groups. All of these have potential for pointing you towards the happy (metal detecting) hunting grounds. They include maps for:

- Amateur geologists, amateur archeologists
- Bikers, dirt-bike riders
- Bird watchers, botany clubs, arboretums
- Gardens, rose gardens, Japanese gardens
- Hikers, campers, nature trails
- History buffs, preservation societies
- Horse trails
- Hunting, fishing fans
- Off-road vehicle enthusiasts
- Outdoor photographers
- Shooting ranges, gun clubs
- Rock climbers

Use these maps and guides to find good places to hunt.

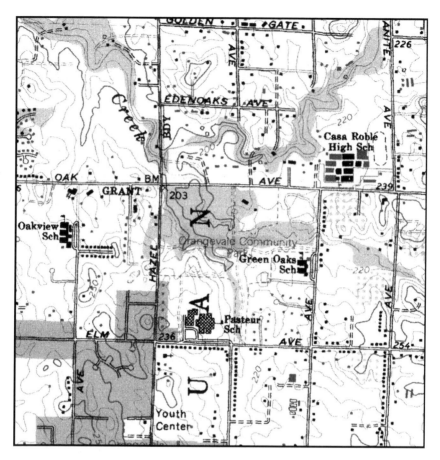

Figure 25. Detail of Topographical map from the US Geological Survey showing schools, campgrounds and parks from 1967.

2. Older paper maps

Old maps are a powerful resource. Take your old map and compare it to a recent street map. Start by marking the schools and parks that were present back in the '60s and see if those places still exist today. If a school was built in 1960 and it's still there today, then that's well over 50 years of people congregating in the same place. That's an excellent place to search for coins. Even if the school was torn down, and now there's an empty lot, that's still a good spot for coin-shooting. If you see a school on

90

the present-day map, and looking at the 1960's map you see there wasn't even a street in that location at that time, then you know the school was built recently. You can still search in the newer school, but don't expect to find a lot of the older coins.

Don't limit yourself to schools and parks either. Look at churches, gathering places, ball fields, and major thoroughfares. Maybe there are a dozen roads and bridges into your town today, but back in the '60s there was only one road, one bridge, and one main street. This is where you will find the richest fields for metal detecting.

Look at the heart of the downtown area where you live. Locate the large open spaces where people would tend to congregate for walks, picnics, or to take the kids. Are you starting to see how valuable a map can be?

3. A personal experience with maps

I live in Folsom, California. It's an old town. When I first got my detector, I found lots of coins, but rarely anything older than the 1970s. Then I found an old USGS Topo map for Folsom dated 1967. Shocking! The whole town was less than a mile long and half a mile wide back then. Everywhere I had been searching was less than 40 years old. Most of it was actually less than 20 years old. No wonder I wasn't finding silver coins! The map showed all the town's activities were in what we now call "Old Town" in Folsom. I started searching these older areas. That made a big difference. The point is, old maps provide a better understanding of where coins might be found.

E. Working the internet

The internet provides a powerful tool for selecting your search sites.

> "I thought of alternate approaches to searching and found what I think is probably the best, no-cost source of information available . . . the internet! This tool will help you dig into the past and more. You will find what used to take weeks or longer now takes only hours to do, and from the comfort of your own home.
>
> I believe that just about every county auditor or assessor in every state of the union has a website available to the public."
>
> - M. Adam Namerow, *Cyber Sleuthing*, W&E Treasures, September, 2003.

1. Current online maps

Internet views are often much more detailed than printed maps. Some examples are MapQuest (http://MapQuest.com) and Google Maps (http://maps.google.com). Be sure to click on the Aerial tab for MapQuest, and the Satellite tab for Google Maps. Use satellite views to supplement your old maps. If a school was present on your old map back in 1965, but it's missing from the current map, then use the satellite view to see what's there now. It may still be a good site to search. Satellite views will also show you entrances, exits, trails, and areas that might be hidden when you are visiting on foot.

Even if you are somewhat familiar with the area you intend to search, it's a good idea to check it out on the internet. You'd be surprised what you can discover. A state park, for example, might charge an entry fee, but there may be a foot path from a residential area where you can hike in and save yourself the parking fee.

You can also find online Topo maps on TerraServer (http://terraserver.com/). As described from their web site:

> "The TerraServer-USA Web site is one of the world's largest online databases, providing free public access to a vast data store of maps and aerial photographs of the United States. TerraServer is designed to work with commonly available computer systems and Web browsers over slow speed communications links."

An aerial view can be seen by going to http://www.bing.com/maps/. When you zoom in to your town, click on the "Bird's Eye" view.

Google Earth is a powerful search tool that will supplement your searching abilities. This program must be downloaded and installed on your computer, and works similar to a Web browser.

With Google Earth you can zoom in on satellite views and take advantage of a number of overlays that add crucial information to your search. For example, Google Earth has a number of tabs that will enable you to click on photographic images that other visitors have uploaded. Google is also in the process of providing ground-level 360-degree images to major cities across the US. This means you can see the site you intend to search both from an aerial view and a ground level view. With Google Earth installed and launched, look in the lower left corner under "Layers." Check the "Street View" box; this will provide access to the 360-degree image, if there is one available. All-in-all, this is a fascinating service that will help you in a number of ways.

Google Earth works with another site, Panoramio, (http://www.panoramio.com), where you can post your own photos. Once Google reviews the photographs you have posted to Panoramio, then they are added to the database of images that Google Earth accesses. Photographs posted by viewers appear as small blue squares on the screen. Clicking on them will open the photograph. If you are wary of installing yet another program on your computer, you can also see both aerial and street level photographs with Panoramio.

Finally, try Trails.com (http://www.trails.com/trails.aspx), which shows popular hiking trails with topographic features. With a little investigative skill, you can find trails that have been around for decades, even pioneer trails, so you can find not only coins, but historic relics as well.

The internet is a great place to find out the age of houses. Simply check out real estate sites. They list the year the house was built. By looking up several houses in one neighborhood, you can tell the decade when that location was first developed.

2. Older online maps

One of the best strategies for selecting good search sites is to get both a current and an old map of your town. Some older maps can be found on the internet, but finding copies of old paper maps is a bit easier. Remember, the US stopped minting those silver dimes and quarters back in 1965, so if you can find a map of what your area looked like back then, you will be well on your way to finding good sites. Try the internet and auction sites, such as eBay (http://www.ebay.com). You can usually find an old road map for under $5.00. If you cannot locate an old street map for your area, a good alternative is to buy what they call a "Topo" (topographical) map from the US Geological Survey (http://topomaps.usgs.gov/index.html). Many of these Topo maps are pretty old, and they show lots of detail, with schools, parks, and campgrounds clearly defined.

You can find old maps at libraries, in history books, and especially on the internet. Try Ebay for old maps of your town. This provides HUGE opportunities.

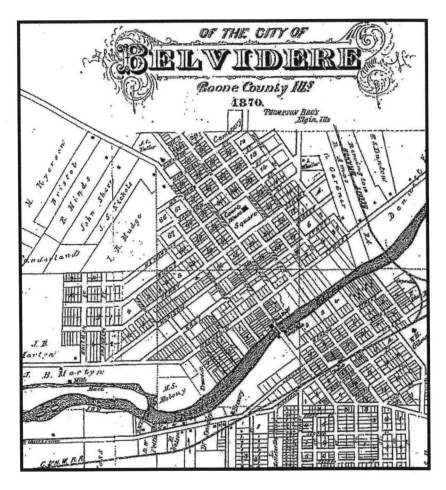

Figure 26. An old "Plat Map" from 1870 is typical of the archival records you can find online.

While we're considering old maps, let's take another look at **Topo maps** which are often available for older dates. A "Topo" map (short for topography) refers to any map showing surface features and elevation, but it most commonly refers to the detailed maps produced by the US Geological Survey over the latter part of the 20th century. Specifically, hikers, campers, and property owners use the most detailed version of these maps, the 7.5 minute scale, for gaining an appreciation of what's on the land. For the metal detectorist, the great value of USGS Topo maps comes from the fact that there are some old versions showing exquisite detail that you can't find from road maps of the same era. Topo maps can be found online, in most map stores, and at US Geological Service offices. They are considered "old" only because most of them were created decades ago.

It definitely pays off to have a Topo map of your home town. If you're lucky, your version may be dated from the 1960s or 1970s, but even more recent maps are useful in showing campgrounds, dry lake beds, and other such geological features sometimes omitted on street maps. Dick Stout covered Topo maps in the August 1991 issue of *Western and Eastern Treasures* magazine, in an article titled *Topographical Maps*, but in those days not as much was available on the internet.

Strictly speaking, you don't absolutely need a hard-copy printed version, as you can find just about anything online nowadays – but it really helps to have the hard copy right in front of you. Just click on any of these commercial sites, to see what your area looks like:

- http://www.mytopo.com/
- http://www.topozone.com/
- http://www.digital-topo-maps.com/

That last URL listing is probably the easiest to use. Just remember, when you have zoomed in to the town level, to click on "MyTopo" (upper right) to see the Topo version. Those and many other map sites will display your local area topography, and if you spend a little time at your computer screen, that may be all you need. They offer to sell the maps to you at a price a little higher than the USGS cost, but the USGS Topo maps are somewhat more valuable since you can see the date it was created and revised.

If you want to buy a Topo map, a reasonably-priced supplier is the USGS, at web site at: http://www.usgs.gov/. Finding and navigating to the specific town you live in, however, can be a nightmare of classic proportions. That's because the USGS Topo maps are organized by older town or neighborhood names, which often have little or no relationship to current names.

If you look on the USGS web site, and look up the name of a large city, you can generally find the right map. If you live in a small town, however, there is no telling what the map name will be - your town or any of the other small villages in the same area. If you live in Wichita, Kansas, for example, you can find that map easily enough. But if you live just east of Wichita, the next map over is Andover, filed under the A's in their index. Go east again, and the next map name is Santa Fe Lake. But there is no such town in that area. There is a Lake Santa Fe Road, and that is where USGS map gets its name.

There IS a way to find these names, but it's a little tedious.
- Go to Map Mart: http://www.mapmart.com/.
- Click on the Services tab, then "topo maps" to see the menu.
- Navigate to the " *1:24,000 - 7.5' or 7 x 9 mile area"* maps for your state. Keep clicking to zoom in on your town. As you get closer you will see the map names written diagonally across a grid.
- You can order the maps from this site or go back to the USGS site and navigate to the correct map using the correct alphabetical map name.

There are several (ever-changing) methods of getting Topo maps from the USGS. You can navigate to the USGS site then print from your computer screen, or simply order the map from their site, as follows:

- Enter http://www.usgs.gov/faq/categories/9797/3571
- Scan the choices. The most helpful link is: http://viewer.nationalmap.gov/viewer/.
- Enter your town name. You will see an on-screen topo map for your area.
- You can print from your screen, or go back and order a hard copy of this map.

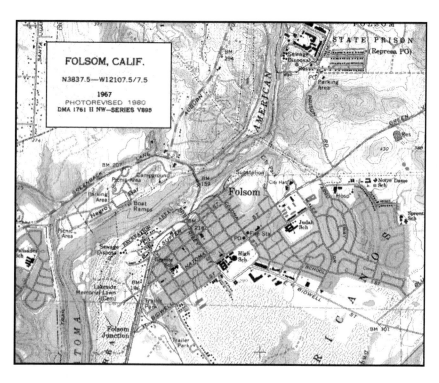

Figure 27. Topo map detail showing schools and creeks.

3. County landownership maps

Another older but more difficult to find map is what is known as County Land Ownership maps, created in the mid 1800s. They preceded the Topo maps, and cover only some of the counties in the US.

If you have hours of spare time and infinite patience you can try to find these maps through government web sites, but it's much faster and easier to use commercial sites, such as: http://mytopo.com/products/privatelands.cfm.

Click on "Enter and address" then zoom in and you'll see the old map, if one is available.

4. Comparing old versus new maps

Once you have both an old and a new map for your area then the fun begins. You can check out which schools, streets, campgrounds, and ball fields were around then, and compare that to a current day map. See which streets were the main thoroughfares. You begin to get an idea of places to search.

Specifically, you can compare the old versus the new for specific landmark features, such as schools and parks (listed on page 89).

You can apply the same old vs. new strategy to the specialty maps too. For example, you can find listings of state and national parks in books from the 1960s on the internet, and compare them to current lists of state and national parks. You can find hiking trail and campground books from 50 years ago, and see what is there now.

One of the most rewarding uses of the new map versus old map comparisons is to locate ghost towns, neighborhoods, or even individual streets and houses that were present a long time ago, but do not appear on the modern map. This is a good indication that the area was cleared or abandoned.

Veteran ghost town researcher Gary B. Speck advises looking at old Rand McNally maps, where the index includes the population figures for many small towns. For more population detail, he suggests getting a copy of the larger Commercial Atlas, if you can, as they are sometimes discarded by libraries for newer editions.

> "That is where the Commercial Atlas comes in. With its listing of all places with a population, suddenly a valuable tool combination is revealed."

- Gary B. Speck, *Ghost Towning with Rand McNally*, W&E Treasures, September, 1990.

A tip from one of the masters of ghost town research:

"Maps are outdated quickly." That little tidbit of knowledge should never be forgotten. . . .The big thing about properly using maps for research is to compare older ones and new ones, as well as maps prepared for various usages - hence the focus above on older ones, and below on various types.

- Gary B. Speck, *How do You Find Ghost Towns*, W&E Treasures, September, 1993.

Some other handy map references:

- https://www.google.com/maps
- http://www.mapmart.com
- http://www.mapquest.com/
- http://maps.nationalgeographic.com/
- http://www.bing.com/maps/
- http://terrafly.com/

See the **Appendix A** as well: ***Metal Detecting Resources***.

F. Historical research

1. History books and newspapers

A campground in the 1950s is now an abandoned lot on state land. A former county fair ground is now split up into a business park and a little used county park. These sites are prime targets for a person with a metal detector. So, how do you find out about such locations? A little bit of historical research goes a long way towards improving your success in metal detecting.

There are many sources of solid information for finding good targets. Most libraries have a large section devoted to local history. You can find out about the people who established your town, the trails and roads that ran through your neighborhood long ago, and the big social events where lots of people were walking around on public land. Valuable leads are available from sports publications, camping information, holiday celebrations, and anything where large groups of people got together for social events.

Besides the library, try your local historic society and civic groups, such as Lions and the Elks Clubs. Get to know the librarians too. They can be quite helpful simply by telling them what you are interested in. In addition to books on history, try looking under camping and hiking in your area. As an example, I found a book on local history that indicated there was a large boarding house at a major intersection in my town. The location is now a car sales lot, and there is a large, wooded walking path beside it. This is the same path the boarding house residents used over 50 years ago, and it's on public land. Just browsing through the books about your town you will come across important clues pointing towards places for you to search.

Figure 28. Almost every town has a Historical Society or even a History Museum.

Another good source is the back issues of magazines, especially treasure hunting magazines. Most of the advice in these articles is timeless. Also, try the sporting, hiking, camping magazines. Look for important social and civic events. Maybe there was a big Boy Scout camp in your area, or a "Revival Meeting" location. With just a little effort, you will find good target areas.

> "Old newspapers can't be beat for researching historical leads, for they are but the voices for their times."
> -   John H. Murrell, *Those Great Old Newspapers*, W&E Treasures, August, 2005

> "Finding old newspapers, reading their offerings, and searching for clues can be educational, interesting, and most important . . . profitable."
>
> -   Dick Stout, *Old News is Good News*, W&E Treasures, December, 1997

Stout recommends looking at the various sections of an old newspaper, the headlines, the obituaries, the social columns, and even the classified ads (such as the lost and found).

2. Library research

Libraries are filled with books on local history. These histories, stories, and memoires are often loaded with leads to help you find old locations to search. Pick up any book on the local history of your town. Look for stories on celebrations, boarding houses, sporting events, local businesses, and the town industry.

Figure 29. A visit to the library pays off in metal detecting research.

This is such a broad topic, it's hard to know where to begin. I'll tell you one of the stories that got me started. Our detecting club has a library of detecting books and local history texts. I picked up one called *Historic Spots in California*, by Mildred Brook Hoover, Hero Eugene Rensche, and Ethel Grace Rehsche. It was written in 1932 with revisions and additions, so the copy I had was printed in 1953.

Scanning the old book at random, I came across this:

Roger's "Shed," a Crossroads Station

About half a mile south of the current village of Sheridan stood a very busy crossroads station during the days of stage coaches and freighters. It was situated on the Sacramento-Nevada road at a point where four other roads diverged: one running westerly to Nicolaus in Sutter County (thirteen miles); one running northwest to Marysville (fifteen miles) via Kempton's Crossing; a third going northeasterly toward Grass Valley (twenty eight miles) via McCourtney's Crossing; and a fourth following easterly to Auburn (twenty miles) via Danetown.

Wow! Is that specific enough for you? The location is described to a tee, and gives a hint at all the traffic that was involved. The story continues:

At this strategic location in 1857, a man named E. C. Rogers built a one-story house with a 150 foot shed in front. The "Shed" - "Union Shed" as it was called - soon became a place of importance. Here the long freight teams which then thronged the roads sought rest and shelter from the summer's heat or the winter's rain, and here the farmers of the surrounding country brought their hay and grain to supply the needs of these same teams.

Figure 30. Historical marker for the Shed, a trading post site found in a history book.

That was one of the first research projects I engaged it. I drove to the site later that same week and found a little town barely clinging to life. Many of the stores were closed, so it was close to becoming a ghost town. There was a historic marker on the site mentioned in the book. The abandoned buildings and empty lots made for some great relic hunting and coin-shooting.

Other books described the local businessmen of my home town, and the major industries. Most historical books describe social events, prominent news stories, leading politicians, and cultural celebrations, and even crime stories. All of these can be used as clues to places to hunt. If nothing else, they tell you where things were happening and when they occurred.

Figure 31. Historic buildings abound in all parts of the country. Here a cabin is preserved as a museum in Fiddletown, California. Historic marker is barely visible at the lower right.

This leads to some suggestions for getting started on research in your location. It's like going to a flea-market. You may not be shopping for anything specific, but when you see what you need, it'll pop out at you. Pick up any historical book at your local library and make note of:

- Abandoned houses, out-of-business industries
- Blacksmiths and boarding of horses
- Boarding houses, saloons, hotels
- Civil war activities and battlefields
- Crime stories, especially unsolved robberies
- Discovery of natural resources that lured people to your town
- Discovery of ores (gold, copper, silver) and assay offices
- Fairgrounds, picnic areas
- Fires, floods, or disasters that destroyed buildings
- Halls and meeting places for civic groups, such as the Elks club, or Grangers.
- Local landmarks and points of interest
- Major places of employment and their locations
- New bridges, ferries, thoroughfares that opened up a community
- School openings, closings
- Sporting events, ball fields, competitions
- Trails and campgrounds
- School openings, closings
- Surveying expeditions, land grants, land sales
- Social events, church events
- Wagon train and emigrant routes

All of these nuggets of information must then be coordinated with your map searches and research from the previous section.

This process, of course, is just the tip of the proverbial iceberg when it comes to finding good areas to hunt. It's more of a "keep your eyes open" approach to discovering opportunities for yourself that are specific to your location. One of the best ways to get ideas for research is to look at past articles in the treasure hunting magazines and books.

Take a look at *Detecting in Deed*, by Lance W. Comfort, in the October, 2008, Vol. 42 issue of *W&E Treasures*. He tells an amazing story of how he used an old property deed and old maps to find a long forgotten cellar hole.

> "Websites can also provide inspiration to those either in a rut or just plain burnt out from unproductive hunting."
>
> - Terry Neils, *Online Tips*, Lost Treasures, May, 2003.

Now, go to the library. See if there is a section on local history. Don't be afraid to ask the research librarian for help. These librarians usually have a degree in library science and will be more than happy to help in your research. Your questions might even "make their day."

Again, this is a stay-alert type of exercise. You will be looking for events, transitions, and conditions that will point to a specific location which increases the odds of you nailing down the location of something of historic or monetary value that you can find with your metal detector.

Figure 32. A local history section is often available at the city library.

I fully expect, when you read the history books and back issues of magazines, that you will be well on your way to writing your own suggestions for unique ways to find locations for lost treasures. It's not that you need to write, but you will benefit tremendously by delving into local history, keeping you mind open for pertinent facts, then piecing together the many clues, until it all comes together into a picture that is custom-designed for your town. It's very much like metal detecting itself. You search and you find.

Another great source of historic information is the specialized library. Besides the good old public library, most towns have specialized repositories of information. In my home town area, Sacramento, California, there are quite a few libraries dedicated to select topics. Here are just some of the libraries in the area that would be useful for research:

- California States Railroad Museum Library
- Crocker Art Museum Gerald Hansen Library
- Geological Survey Library
- California State Department of Transportation Library
- Lavender Library, Archives and Cultural Exchange
- Turn Verein German-American Cultural Center Library
- Roseville Genealogical Society Library
- Sacramento Family History Center
- Sacramento Italian Cultural Society Library
- Women's Resource Center, Lioness Library

The same kinds of specialized resources are spread across the country. When visiting a library, be sure to take advantage of the research library or other staff members who can help guide your search for good detecting sites. Even the volunteers, docents, and ushers usually have inside information that can be useful to you. Don't be shy about asking for help with your specific metal detecting goals.

3. Where people congregated

Remember the Rule of Thumb: "Search where lots of people have walked." The best place to search for coins and valuables is where large numbers of people have congregated. The amount of treasure you will find is directly related to the number of people who have been there, and for how long. You could almost make a formula out of it:

Loot = People x Time

That is, the amount of **Loot** is equal to the number of **People** times the amount of **Time** they spent there. Of course you will have to subtract out the coins that are no longer available because of other coin-shooters, or due to them being covered up by paving or landscaping.

Schools, parks, churches, and public meeting places, then, are good hunting grounds. Most metal detecting clubs will target parks and schools. Also consider bike paths, hiking trails, campgrounds, sports fields, fishing holes, playgrounds, outdoor concert locations, and roadside vending stands. You start to get the general idea. Then you begin to think strategically every time you are out for a drive or a walk, and you start recording prime hunting sites in that big filing cabinet inside your head.

4. Trails and ghost towns

Many locations that were popular a while back may be forgotten, little used, or even abandoned in the present. What were the roads and trails used by explorers when your area was being settled? Are the same roads in use today? Are there any abandoned farms, mining towns, or old airports in your area?

Try to imagine what the roads were like before the highway was put in. Did the horses use the same path that the cars use now? In some locations you can see the old horse and buggy trail next to the freeway where the old timers would travel. Modern highway construction did not follow the same path, because the highway has to have wide sweeping turns, whereas the horses could take a more meandering route. In your travels, keep an eye out for the old roads. Use maps and publications to ferret out ghost towns and abandoned properties in your area. Soon you will develop an eye, like a photographer, for sites that were busy in the past and make for good hunting in the present.

It is MUCH better to discover your own ghost towns, comparing old against new maps, than to try to rely of public listings of over-publicized ghost towns. See Comparing old versus new maps, page 100. Look for abandoned sites, dead industries, forgotten trails, and long-lost locations of group gatherings,

Figure 33. What historic markers can you find in your neck of the woods? This Pony Express trail marker is located near the California-Nevada border.

5. The Civil War

If you are fortunate enough to live in a state where Civil War battles took place then you have the added advantage in treasure hunting to add some classic relics to your collection. The Civil War, and the artifacts that accompanied it, constitutes an entire subculture for treasure hunters. There are books and catalogs describing the bullets, buckles, and buttons that are common from that era. The online forums include Civil War relics as a special category. Many modern detectors have a "Relic Mode" to help you find metal objects from the past.

6. Buried treasure

Finding buried treasure or a hidden cache is "The Big One" in metal detecting. Who doesn't dream of instant wealth? In fact, there are books and magazines dedicated to that very idea. Don't get your hopes up, however! There are over 320 million people in the United States. If you scour the newspapers and the internet, you will find only a handful of stories of people finding a hidden treasure in any given year. The odds are much worse than a million to one that you will find The Big One.

You WILL, however, find plenty of things with your metal detector. Your pockets will bulge with coins, jewelry, and small treasures. Ship and pirate treasures can be found nowadays, but the process is often quite expensive. Billionaires and corporations with recovery ships and dedicated underwater detecting scanners may employ a small army of divers and historians to locate the big treasures. This however is far beyond the capacity of a lone hobbyist with a $300 detector. It's probably better to content yourself with the goal of finding an occasional silver or gold coin, and keep an open mind. If Providence really wants to make you an instant millionaire, then you can trust in the machinations of a purposeful universe, but just don't hold your breath while you're waiting!

G. Unusual places

1. Hiding spots

People often hide their belongings. During the Great Depression, when families could not trust their finances to a bank, they would often store their valuables in hiding places for safe-keeping. Likewise, when our nation was largely rural, folks couldn't always ride into town to store things in a bank. They would use loose planks in the floor, movable bricks in a wall, or stones in a rock fence to hide cash, jewelry, or other possessions. Sometimes, such as with a flood, a fire, or sudden death, the owner would not be able to recover his belongings. Keep an eye out, especially in older homesteads, for common hiding places.

Look up the back issues of some of the treasure hunting magazines and you'll find all sorts of specialty search sites to add to your repertoire. Consider fence post holes, wells, hollow trees, inside walls, under porches, inside barns and tool sheds.

2. Discards

How many times have you been vacuuming, either in your house or in your car, when you hear a loud clunking sound and you wondered, "What was that?" How many times was it a quarter, or perhaps a ring, or earring? Vacuum cleaner bags probably contain a fortune, although few people would go there. Some gas stations now have industrial sized vacuum cleaners, and these too will be sucking up lots of coins. Some enterprising treasure hunters will go to gas stations and check car wash drains and vacuum canisters. Along the same lines, people will search in car junk yards, old vending machines, and thrift stores. The point is, treasure is where you find it.

3. Urban hunting

In most towns the oldest areas and the newest areas are in the same place. Cities and towns generally grow from the center outwards, but the oldest structures then get demolished so that new down-town buildings can be constructed.

The key to finding old coins and artifacts in a metropolitan setting is to focus in on these old areas. You soon find out, however, that there are few decent places to hunt in the center of the city. There are often too many office buildings, commercial properties, and lack of open space. Aside from a few parks, it's hard to find a place to go metal detecting.

There are several ways to get around this roadblock, and the main three methods can be summarized as Micro-site Selection, Private Property Permission, and Transient Opportunity Utilization.

a) Micro-site selection.
   Even in the most densely urbanized cities there are small grassy areas by the curb, center strips on the boulevard, and dirt pathways between buildings that may be ideal places to hunt with your metal detector. The trick here is to find those precious areas that have escaped the bulldozer and landscaper for the past 50 years or so. This takes some detective work, but there are simple ways to assess whether you have a chance or not of finding something old. Is the grass perfectly manicured and surrounded by recent brickwork or masonry? Or is it full of weeds, down-trodden and neglected? You will recognize it when you find spaces that have not been dug up, filled in, or plastered over in the last few decades. This is where you want to hunt.

b) Private Property Permission,

Many of the good hunting sites in urban areas are on private property. This is a barrier for many hobbyists, as asking and getting permission to hunt is viewed as difficult. The truth is, however, that most people are kind and generous, and they are more than willing to cooperate. The real difficulty is in finding and getting in contact with the owner. This often requires that you speak with a building manager, maintenance staff personnel, or security guard. They may even serve as the go-between for getting permission. Such employees will need to know what you are doing anyway. Their concern is usually not your hunting, but that you leave the ground clean and the grass undisturbed when you are finished. Once you have your first success in asking for and getting permission to search on private property, you begin to realize what vast opportunities await you by the simple act of asking.

A good time to seek permission on private property is when the land is being sold or renovated. This brings us to the next tool in your search, the transient opportunity.

c) Transient Opportunity Utilization.

Transient opportunities are those situations where a normally off-limits site suddenly or temporarily becomes available for hunting. This might be the city tearing up a sidewalk, a fire destroying a building, the utility company laying new pipe, or a landscaper tearing out old trees.

Figure 34. Park land is being bulldozed to put in a new bike path. The bare ground provides a transient opportunity for metal detecting.

If you travel the same streets every day, or if you are familiar with a certain section of your town, you can easily train yourself to recognize the opportunities as they become available. An old street near me was getting torn up so they city could install fiber optic cables. Many long sections of the shoulder of this road were covered with bushes and scrub trees. The vegetation had to be cleared out before they could dig the trench for the cable. There was a week-long period where the shrubbery was removed but they had not yet started digging. I took my detector out there and found many old coins. The next week they dug the trench, laid the cable and filled the trench back in. Now, soil that was once 5 feet underground was on the top. I searched again and found more coins. The next week they covered the area with asphalt. The transient opportunity lasted just 2 weeks.

Now don't look for long lists of possible opportunities. Instead, stay alert to changes in the landscape in your home town. You might read in the newspaper that the city is going to drain that pond in the downtown park for maintenance. Transient opportunity.

You hear from a neighbor that the Elks Club is finally going to tear down that old, leaky dance hall and build a new structure. Transient opportunity.

You see on the local news that the High School is going to clear a field and lay down astro-turf for a ball park. The first step is to level off a foot of top soil. Transient opportunity.

Soon you realize there are plenty of chances, plenty of places to hunt in the downtown area. Teach your hunting buddies how to spot these opportunities. You'll have more than enough to keep you busy.

These are just the main categories for urban hunting. There are many other sources for good hunting possibilities. Stay alert for once-a-year events, such as parades that assemble on grassy areas, or craft fairs where people congregate. Just because your downtown area is covered with office buildings doesn't mean there are no places to hunt.

4. More tips and tricks

Here are some things the experts recommend:

"Road construction crews are a great source of information. You may discover that one of your favorite parks is being graded, or that a new road is being cut into an old park, exposing some deep coins for a day or two."

- Daniel J. Dictus, *Thinking Like a Treasure Hunter*, W&E Treasures, June, 1996.

Look around parking meters.
Look around bus benches.
Look around telephone booths.
Find out where cabs stop to pick up passengers.
The grassy areas around bank walk-up windows and automatic teller machines.
Look around flagpoles.
Check out drive-up windows.
Bicycle racks in schools, playgrounds, transit stations.
Look around vending machines, newspaper dispensers.

- Mark C. Blazek, *10 Great Places to Coinshoot*, W&E Treasures, July, 1987

Rallies, musical events, political gatherings, religious meetings - all these have a central area of interest, with a standing or seated congregation of people around that central point.

- H. Glen Carson, *Patterns of Lost Objects*, W&E Treasures, February, 1995.

Figure 35. Outdoor events, such as concerts in the park or soccer tournaments, provide a great opportunity for metal detecting.

H. Unusual methods

<u>1. Dowsing</u>

You'll see advertisements in some of the hobby magazines for dowsing rods or remote sensing instruments. The claims seem odd, like voodoo science. Yet, you'll find plenty of people who swear by these methods.

When I was a young boy, a friend showed me how to cut a Y-shaped branch, strip the bark off the top ends of the Y, and then twist them like you were revving up a motorcycle. My friend then had me walk across a sloping field, and to tell him when I felt something. About 20 yards into the field, the bottom stem of the branch started pulling down as if I had a fish on the line. Taking another few steps, the tugging stopped. Coming back again across the same spot, the tugging was apparent again. My friend then took me to the top end of the field and showed me the control valve for a water pipe. You guessed it; the water pipe ran under the field exactly where I felt the tugging.

They used to call that "water witching," and not too long ago people used that technique to decide where to drill for water.

Years later, I tried a similar experiment myself, using two L-shaped steel rods. I couldn't see or feel anything. The big question is whether or not such methods work. Bottom line: you have to judge for yourself. I do find, though, that it's wise to keep an open mind on such subjects. There is a whole universe of knowledge that we may not have yet tapped into. Maybe it's some form of psychic ability, or maybe there is a mechanism at work that we are not aware of.

If you do decide to try dowsing, I would suggest you start by experimenting with your own home-made dowsing rods. You can find instructions on the Internet on how to make them, and how to use them. Then, if you have success with your home-made instruments, you might feel better about investing in a commercial version. I would NOT recommend that you run out and spend hundreds of dollars on a manufactured instrument with the expectation that it will bring you instant wealth. That's called gullibility. On the other hand, if you have success with home-made or primitive dowsing rods, then perhaps you have a knack for it. In that case, taking the risk of buying a commercial instrument may be more justifiable.

2. Coin roll hunting.

You go to a bank. You ask them for rolls of dimes – maybe $100 worth. You go home and open the rolls. You look for silver dimes, or any coins that might have value to collectors. That is what coin roll hunting is all about. The silver dimes are worth much more than their face value, based on their silver content. The same can be done for half dollars, quarters, nickels, and pennies.

The US Mint stopped producing silver dimes back in 1965, and since then people have been seeking them, so that now there are very few left in circulation. Even if you sort through $100 worth of dimes, you still have only a slim chance of finding real silver. But, since the process is relatively simple, and you can always just turn in the coins again, many people enjoy the process. The best rolls to search are half-dollar coins, as there are so few in circulation, and historically people have not been as actively seeking them for their silver content. As with dimes, half dollars changed from 90% silver to a copper laminate, or "clad" coin, in 1965. Fortunately for collectors, the Kennedy half dollar continued to contain silver, at 40%, between 1965 and 1970.

Quoting from Wikipedia:
(http://en.wikipedia.org/wiki/Half_dollar_(United_States_coin)

> "The value of silver had risen by 1962-63 to the point that it became worthwhile to melt down U.S. coins for their bullion value. U.S. Silver coins (those of ten cent value and above, which contained 90% silver through 1964) began to disappear from circulation, leading the United States to change to layered composition coins made of a copper core laminated between two cupro-nickel outer faces for the 1965 - present coinage years. The Kennedy half-dollar design, however, continued to be minted in a 40% silver-clad composition from 1965–1970."

If you decide you want to try your hand at coin roll hunting, be sure to read the literature and the online forums, as there are important exceptions to the general guidelines described above. You will also want to become familiar with the various coin dates, mint marks, and relative value of the denominations you will be searching.

3. Magnetics

Some science supply catalogs sell large magnets encased in rubber that you can tie a string to and dip in the water from a bridge. Every once in a while you might find something with that method, either from a dock, the side of a pond, or even in the ocean. Nowadays, you can purchase very powerful rare earth magnets that are capable of hauling in many pounds of junk. Err! . . . make that treasure. Enterprising people will sometimes make a long rack of such magnets and drag it across a field to pick up iron objects. This does not work with most coins, but it is good for the metals that are attracted to magnets. This includes meteorites too. Magnets mounted on a bar behind a jeep will effectively retrieve meteorites in a "strewn field," which is a location where a meteorite is known to have broken up.

Figure 36. File under unusual devices: A home-made magnetic pickup device constructed from powerful rare earth magnets in PVC piping, pulled by a luggage rack.

4. Transient and Unusual Opportunities

Transient opportunities are those circumstances that arise every so often that provide a temporary advantage for the treasure hunters. (See the above section F 7 on Urban Hunting.) This may include such events as:
- New construction
- Fires
- Grading and landscaping
- Abandoned property
- Detours
- Draining of lakes or ponds

If you can keep an eye open for such opportunities, you will have an ever-new source of search sites.

Try hunting when the ground begins to thaw:

Water is a better conductor of RF signals than dry soil, so the saturated ground carries the impulses from your coil deeper and also returns the signal from any target that you find with a solid sound in your headphones.

- Lou Anderson, *The Spring Thaws Make Good Coin Hunting*, W&E Treasures, May, 1983.

John R. Kongsvik describes the opportunities created from sand being shifted around by a hurricane.

"The dunes were gone, along with all the sand that was banked up against the famous boardwalk," *The Storm Surge*, W&E Treasures, July, 2000

Look for temporarily drained swamps, ponds, reservoirs, and lakes. H. Glenn Carson tells of a fellow who donned snowshoes and walked on the sticky muck of a drained reservoir to find a bunch of old coins:
Better Finds in Better Locations, W&E Treasures, October, 2005.

7. Hunting for People

A. When you're hunting alone

You're never really alone. No matter where you go there will be a land owner, a park ranger, a groundskeeper, or a neighbor who has a legitimate interest in what you are doing. There's an unfortunate tendency to think these people will somehow interfere with your treasure hunting, but the fact is they are valuable assets in your quest, and the right attitude will pay off in the long run.

As an example, when I first started hunting, I was wary of strangers, but I had gone to a park with another treasure hunter from the club. Rather than shy away from the park maintenance man, my friend ambled up to him and explained what we were looking for. The park worker was very cooperative and he pointed out the location where a private home was once located on the park lands. The house had burned down many years ago, and he showed us the location. We found a number of old coins, artifacts, and household items thanks to his friendliness.

Develop a friendly disposition yourself, and interact cordially with other people you come across. Very rarely will you encounter any hostility. The norm is to spark the curiosity of the people you meet. With just a little effort on your part, you can turn the situation to your advantage.

B. Owners – getting permission

You need permission to hunt on private land. Getting that permission is easier than you think. You can knock on doors, leave a card, or even send a letter to the owner of a place you think is good for hunting. Some treasure hunters offer to turn over any jewelry they find to the owner, while the hunter keeps all the coins. Others will split the finds with the land owner. Be sure to protect their property and refill the holes from digging.

C. Working with partners

There's power in numbers. Hunting with a partner has several advantages. There may be safety concerns, or if one of you gets injured, it's great to have a helper. One detectorist is generally more experienced than the other, and they can help each other. The other person's detector may provide a second opinion on whether or not to dig a target.

Some of the advantages of working with a partner:

- You save on gas.
- It's safer.
- You have someone to bounce ideas off of with regards to location, strategy, and techniques.
- The other guy will usually have the towel, the band aid, or the digging tool that you forgot.
- Someone is there to say "Oh, nice find!"

D. Metal detecting clubs

1. Joining a local club

Just about every area of the country has a metal detecting club. These are great places to meet hunting buddies and participate in group activities. Joining a local club is an excellent way to advance your enjoyment of this hobby. Generally clubs have discounts on detecting equipment, instructional and educational presentations from seasoned veterans, and opportunities for group hunts. You will easily make new friends and have people to call if you want a companion to go out detecting with.

For a club in your local area, see any of the links below. You can also try a search on the internet using the keywords of your home town and the words "metal detecting club."

- Go Metal Detecting: http://gometaldetecting.com/links-clubs.htm
- Kelly Co.: http://www.kellycodetectors.com/clubs/
- DMOZ Open Directory: http://www.dmoz.org/Recreation/Outdoors/Metal_Detecting/Organizations/
- Friendly Forum: http://metaldetectingforum.com/showthread.php?t=14013
- Metal Detecting clubs: http://www.metaldetectingclubs.org/

Figure 37. Joining a club multiplies your fun. Here club members compare finds after a hunt.

2. National clubs

The major national organizations are listed below.
The Federation of Metal Detector and Archaeological Clubs (FMDAC)

Their website is: http://www.fmdac.org/.

"The Federation of Metal Detector and Archaeological Clubs (FMDAC) was organized in 1984 as a legislative and educational organization to help combat the negative publicity related to the hobby."

FMDAC Purpose

- To unite, promote and encourage the establishment of metal detecting clubs.
- To preserve the sport / hobby of recreational metal detecting and prospecting.
- To make available to FMDAC clubs and Independent members information pertaining to the hobby and to keep members informed as to active legislation

World Wide Association of Treasure Seekers

Their website is: http://www.wwats.org/.

"Our Mission Statement: Preserve, Promote and Protect the right to the use of the Land and Natural Resources for "We the People" now and in the future."

E. Club hunts

Club hunts are group activities. Some club hunts are regularly scheduled trips to local parks, schools, and public lands. Others have seeded hunts where coins and tokens are hidden in a defined area and club members search them out. Still other hunts may be annual events where there is a combination of activities and prizes are given away based on what you find. All-in-all, these activities are loads of fun and provide interesting opportunities for the treasure hunter.

Figure 38. A club is a great way to meet friends.

8. Metal Detecting Technique

You *will* find lots of little treasures. That's easy. The trick, though, is to find lots of coins, valuable jewelry, and precious historic relics, and to find them in an efficient and timely manner. The paragraphs that follow will, hopefully, help you improve your treasure hunting techniques, to improve the amount and quality of the things you find.

A. The art of site selection

1. Go where the valuables are

Good site selection improves your treasure hunting. Most of the stories in treasure hunting magazines involve tricks, hints, and techniques to find good locations to hunt. Use your brain to figure out hot spots in your area. Sure, parks and schools are usually good, but what about that strip of grass between the sidewalk and the curb in the old section of town? What about the old site where the county fairgrounds used to be back in the 1950s?

Figure 39. A park with picnic tables and a play area represents a good area to find coins.

Go where people have congregated in the past, where they lived, where they walked, played, and picnicked. I'll repeat the earlier Rule of Thumb: "Search where lots of people have walked."

Hint: Every time you go out for a hunt, make a record of the coins you found and their dates. Circle the ones that are earlier than 1965, when silver coins were still being minted. In a few months you'll have a record of the best digging sites in your area.

Finally, check out old copies of the metal detecting magazines. Sometimes just reading the titles of the articles will give you clues on where to hunt.

2. A note on the "virgin site"

Soon after you start detecting you will come across what we call a "virgin site." This is an area that has not been searched by anyone with a metal detector, or at least not in the recent past. You can tell you're on a virgin site when you start finding lots of coins and little treasures, and many of the coins are right on the surface. If you're lucky, and this occurs on a high traffic site, you are sure to bring home a good amount of treasure. The key here is to take your time and search thoroughly. It's better to cover 10 square feet carefully than to race across 30 square feet haphazardly. You can then make a note of the exact location you have searched, and come back later and cover the rest of the area.

B. Real time site evaluation

Once you have selected an area to search, take a few minutes to size it up. Where are the oldest trees? Is this a place where folks would relax in the shade on a sunny day? Is the area covered with sod? Landscaping and new grass can add several inches to the ground, making it more difficult to dig down to where the older coins are located. Is there an area that has not been landscaped?

Look at how people enter and exit the site. When I go on a group hunt to a school, everyone seems to prefer searching the ball field. Maybe half the students are ever on the ball field, but 100% of them use the main entry and exit, and there is a grassy area right next to both entrances. That will have the most treasure. Where do people walk? A woman with a baby carriage is going to be on a flat, straight path, not on a steep hillside. Where would kids play in this area? Maybe they are drawn to that low-hanging branch, or that prominent boulder.

Look around. Where are people milling around? If you were to bring your family to visit this place, where would you spread a picnic blanket? Where is the grass worn down from foot traffic? Where would you like to sit just to enjoy the scenery? Perhaps it's on top of a hill overlooking a pond, or by the park bench. All these are clues to finding places to hunt.

C. The art of detector scanning

When you get to a site, set up a grid system or some other method that ensures you're not covering the same area twice. On a playground, for example, you might want to circle around the perimeter, and work your way inward.

If you are searching a baseball field, where would you search first? Where would most spectators congregate? Maybe it's behind home plate, or perhaps between home plate and first base. Where is the grass matted down and worn away by the traffic? Soon, you'll get into a habit of assessing where to search for your best chances of finding coins.

Many detecting enthusiasts use a grid system to scan a particular geographic location. This provides the knowledge and satisfaction that a particular site was well covered for that time period.

That said, there is really no "right way" to cover a site. Some people are perfectly happy to hunt with no systematic coverage of the ground, preferring instead to just follow their nose and hope for the best. They too will find treasures.

Figure 40. Search the heavy traffic areas first, such as in front of the park bench.

D. Equipment and settings

1. Detector settings

Remember to adjust the settings on your detector every time you
go out. Read your User Manual again. Some sites have electrical
interference and you might have to lower the sensitivity. Some
places have lots of junk which may require setting the
discrimination dial to a different level.

Develop your skill in adjusting the discrimination dial. When the
discriminator is set to a low value, you will eliminate junk
metals. As you tune it higher you will reject signals from those
pesky aluminum pull-tabs, but you will begin to lose important
jewelry items as well. It is the mid-range discrimination level
that is difficult to fathom. An expert on the subject says:

> "Because gold and aluminum, which fall in this mid-range,
> are so close in conductivity it's virtually impossible to reject
> one without rejecting the other. This means that some gold
> rings and gold coins will be eliminated if you set your disc
> control to reject aluminum."

> - Dick Stout, *The New Metal Detecting; the Hobby*

One solution is to keep the discrimination setting low, so you
accept aluminum targets, then you can decide on a case-by-case
basis if you think this location is full or junk, or if there is a good
chance of jewelry being located there.

Consider what you are finding too. If there is a lot of trash in the
area, maybe you want to consider a smaller coil, so you can pin-
point the good stuff. Maybe the coins are all deep, and you need
a larger coil. You may benefit from a hand-held pin-pointer.
Some hand-held units are very sensitive and will make short
work of retrieving the coins which your detector discovers.

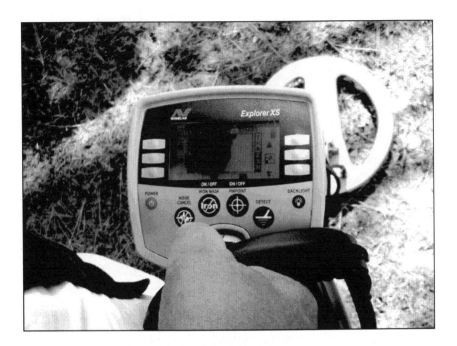

Figure 41. Read your user manual so you know how to adjust detector settings. The Minelab Explorer series of detectors has advanced discrimination features.

2. The art of the beep

Learn to recognize the sounds your detector makes. You've probably noticed by now that a coin generally has a solid and repeatable signal, whereas junk gives a broken, clipped sound that changes every time you scan it. Pull-tabs are not symmetrical. They give one reading when you first scan it, and the signal will then change when you turn 90 degrees.

Learn the coin sounds. Coins will usually register the same value when you turn and scan from a different direction. Learn how that sound differs for the same coin at different depths.

A choppy, broken "bidda-bip-bip" sound occurs more often on junk targets, such as pull-tabs and iron, whereas legitimate coins produce a single solid, repeatable sound. This is hard to describe, but when you hear it, you'll know it: the coin sound will generally start and stop suddenly, going quickly from silent to full volume, and back down to silent again, like a "pow, pow, pow" sound with each sweep of the coil.

Pull-tabs and other asymmetrical items will sometimes give a different reading depending on direction. Going east to west, for example may give a solid signal, while going back from west to east may give something else. This is a strong indication you are scanning an odd-shaped object. That is often, but not always, a junk item.

If you're getting a lot of chatter, or static noise in your headphones, check that you are not under some power lines or near a transformer. You may have to adjust the sensitivity down in order to operate in such areas. Be aware that many electrical transmissions lines are now underground in urban environments.

Other strong indications you are scanning junk: the signal gives one value on the left-to-right swing, and another on the right-to-left swing. A junk signal will often rise and die out slowly.

3. In the field

The style for swinging your detector is a matter of personal choice. Remember, though, that the search field on a circular coil will be cone shaped, so if the swings are farther apart than the coil diameter, then you are missing large areas at the deepest levels. It's best, then to have an overlapping sweep area. Along these same lines, my personal choice it to use a "D-D" style coil. This creates a search area that is closer to a spade shape than the cone shape you get with a circular coil. Now when you swing the coil across any given area you can cover more of the deeper areas with each sweep.

Figure 42. Typical D-D coil shapes are shown here. See Figure 18 for the flattened search-field profile for this type of coil, page 68.

The often rapid pace of scanning with your detector underscores the importance of slowing down once you hear even the slightest beep. Go back and scan the area again, this time with lots of overlap, and swings that are only an inch or two apart. Turn your body 90-degrees and scan again until you have a lock on the location with a pin-pointer.

On site recommendations:

- When detecting on a hillside, hold the detector in the arm that faces the down-slope. It's much easier.

- Set up a grid pattern or other system for scanning your area. Missing large areas of a park, or unknowingly doubling over the same section, makes for inefficient searching. You might want to cover the area in linear fashion, like yard lines on a football field, or make concentric circles from the outer perimeter inward.

- Identify the dates of coins as you find them. You benefit from knowing if you are in an area that might contain silver coins. If you are getting pennies from the 1940s and 1950s, there's a good chance you will also find silver there. If you've found over 10 coins and all of them are 1990 to the present, well, that's a clue too.

- Use your eyes as well as your ears as you search. Many times you can see coins and jewelry right on top of the ground even before your detector picks it up.

"I feel that it is equally important that I keep my eyes carefully scanning the area ahead and to the sides of the ground that the coil is covering. As we all know, the coil can only cover a very small percentage of the ground."

- Frank J. Colletti, *Watch Where You're Searching*, W&E Treasures, December, 1995.

Pick up the trash as you go. This is good for the environment and for other detectorists.

"Most folks who hunt the beach throw the trash back into the sand. I see the same people, hunting the same beach, detecting the same trash and throwing it back every time they go."
- William Lahr, *How to Recover Your Finds*, W&E Treasures, October, 1985.

Keep yourself comfortable. You may be detecting for hours as the environment changes. Don't freeze or sweat too long before you decide to make a change of clothing, get a drink of water, or otherwise give yourself a break.

Keep your gear from annoying you. If the headset is hurting your ears, adjust the spring. If your digging tool is stabbing you in the leg every time you bend down, then move it to a safer location.

E. Digging and lawn care

Soil conditions and the depth of coins will generally determine what kind of digging tools you'll need. Some locations require just a probe and a screwdriver. Others may require a small hand shovel, while really old relics could demand a spade or post-hole digger. Bring the right equipment.

> **CAUTION:** Never stick your hand into the hole you are digging to feel around. Often the "coin" is a piece of jagged metal, and you can suffer a nasty cut quite easily. Instead, use your digging tool to bring the material to the surface, and wear gloves.

Your individual digging style will depend on the soil type in your area. Most detectorists prefer the sod plug or "flap" method of digging up a coin. Here you use a trowel or Lesche tool to punch three sides of a square into the grass, going about 3 or 4 inches deep, then you use the tool to lift the flap up to expose the hole. This leaves one side of the square attached to the rest of the grass, so at least some of the roots remain intact, which means it will grow back easily. You then use a handheld probe to search for the coin, or simply dig more carefully with the digging tool until you spot the target.

If the coin cannot be found by simply lifting the flap, then you will have to search the flap itself for the coin, look into the hole for it, or dig even deeper. You will need to search the walls of the excavation as well. Here is a good point to pull out a small towel or sheet of plastic, then dump any of the loose dirt onto that surface, so you can just pour it back into the hole when you are done, and it leaves the grass pretty close to the way you found it. You don't want to just throw that dirt onto the grass next to the hole, because no amount of scraping and scooping is going to be able to get it back in the ground.

In sandy soils with few rocks, some people prefer using an ice pick or other narrow probe to help locate the coin before digging.

Many areas have hard-pan or clay soil, and the coins are generally found closer to the surface than in sandy soils. In such a case a narrow screwdriver may be sufficient for digging, as many of the coins can be located with the hand-held pin-pointer, or by using the pin-point feature on the detector.

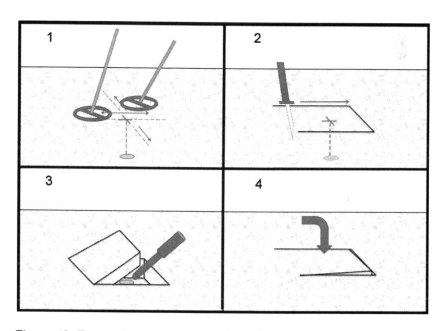

Figure 43. Flap method; use a tool with inch marks, a serrated edge, and a flat top. 1. Scan one direction then perpendicular. 2. Cut three sides of a square around the target. 3. Flip up the plug onto a towel and scan with a hand-held probe. 4. Replace the plug and tamp down the dirt so it looks untouched.

Recent improvements in hand-held detector probes enable you to precisely locate the coin position, sometimes even before you start digging. This enables you to use a smaller digging tool, such as a garden weeder tool. This translates to smaller holes and less damage to the lawn.

There are multiple variations on digging and it will evolve for you and the soil type in your area. YouTube.com has some great videos showing unique digging techniques. No one size fits all situations; just keep in mind that you want the ground to look pretty much untouched when you leave it.

F. Removing the coin

When digging, look for the "impression image." This is the mirror image of a coin impressed in the dirt. You'll see a perfectly round indentation in a clump of soil, where it was resting against the target. It means you have taken the top off the mold formed around the coin. The target then is usually right at the bottom of the hole you just made.

The value of a coin deteriorates if you scratch it. So removing the coin from the surround dirt takes care. Be careful not to scratch the coin with your digging tool. You avoid scratches by digging below the level of the coin and pushing it up to the surface.

Gently break up the clumps of dirt until you find the coin. Again the hand-held pin-pointer is very helpful. ***Do not rub the coin between your fingers.*** Most soils contain a lot of sand and silica which will scratch the surface.

Once you've retrieved the coin, go over the hole once again with the detector. Many coins are part of a "pocket spill" and will have a few "companions."

Many of the coins you find will be valuable collector items. Coin collecting is a separate but parallel hobby to metal detecting. It would benefit you to know how coins are graded, which, in part, determines their value. Coins are graded as follows:

- Mint: "Unc".
- Extremely fine: "XF".
- Very fine: "VF".
- Fine: "F".
- Very good: "VG".
- Good: "G".
- Almost Good: "AG".
- Fair: "Fair"

Finding coins in the ground almost guarantees the coins will be degraded and therefore they will fall into the lower four groups. For more detail on these definitions, see the grading system standards at http://www.acoin.com/grading.htm, or http://en.wikipedia.org/wiki/Coin_grading.

G. When to give up

Sometimes you get a good signal and you simply cannot find the coin. Soon, if you're like most of us, you'll have a foot-wide cavern going down 18 inches and still nothing to show for it. Such excavations not only destroy property, but waste a lot of valuable time, when the target might be just an old sprinkler head or some other junk. Try to avoid that. Give yourself permission to stop digging and move on.

H. Field storage

Many hobbyists use a tool belt or multi-pocket apron to store their collections while in the field. It pays to have one pocket for coins and another for trash, or larger items. You may want multiple small plastic bags to sort your finds until you get home. Many searchers bring along a small water bottle with soapy water as a kind of rough cleaning even before they get home. Make sure there are no holes in your pockets!

I. Learning as you go

Experiment with different discrimination settings. For example, set the discrimination fairly high, so all you're finding is pennies, dimes, and quarters. Are you finding fewer coins? Is it worth your while to have the higher value coins even though you might be missing nickels and rings? For some people, finding more pennies, even if they are corroded zinc coins, is more rewarding than searching for higher phase-shift silver coins. You have to experiment for yourself, to see what you are comfortable with.

When you first start detecting, it's wise to dig everything. See what signals refer to junk and which one are real coins.

As you grow to learn your detector responses, consider NOT digging all signals. On my machine, a Visual Display Identification number (VDI) of 37 is ALWAYS a pull-tab. After digging up about 1000 signals at 37, not one of them was anything else but a pull-tab. On the other hand, a VDI of 22 was sometimes a nickel and sometimes a pull-tab. I still dig all of them. A VDI of 18 is almost always a nickel.

If you get a borderline signal, which could be either a nickel or a pull-tab, then step back and scan the area again from a different angle. Pull-tabs are asymmetrical, and will often give one reading when you scan it east and west, as opposed to north and south.

If your detector uses VDI numbers, be sure you know the values for all the major coins. Metal detecting forums on the internet often include lists of what the TID or VDI number correspond to for various detectors.

Understand that Target Identification (TID) is not always accurate. Junk items often appear as coins - what might be called a false positive. For example, a bottle cap may appear to be a quarter on your display. The other type of error, the false negative, in my opinion occurs less frequently; that is, a quarter appearing as a bottle cap.

Re-examine your choice of coil. A larger coil will generally go deeper, but a smaller one will help you sort out junk in trashy areas.

Consider a D-D coil. These coils flatten the search field, so it's more like the blade of a shovel. This will help you in pin-pointing and the blade will generally go deeper than the same sized round coil.

In addition to the user manual, see if there is a specialty book for your detector. These dedicated texts go into much more detail than the user manual, and you benefit from the expertise of the writer. Some examples follow:

- *The Minelab Explorer & E-Trac Handbook* by Andy Sabich.
- *Spectrum Secrets Third Edition*, by Kevin Mulrooney.
- *Spectrum XLT Engineering Report*, by Mark Rowan.
- *XLT Ring Enhancement Programs*, by Clive James Clynick.
- *Finding Gold, Silver and Coins with the Minelab Sovereign and Excalibur* by Clive James Clynick.

- *Advanced Methods for Finding Gold in the Water with the MineLab Excalibur*, by Clive James Clynick.
- *DFX: From Beginner to Advanced*, by Clive James Clynick.
- *Understanding White's DFX*, by Clive James Clynick.
- *XLT Methods and Custom Programs*, by Clive James Clynick.

There are also books on general metal detecting - too numerous to list, but as an example, see *Coin Hunting . . . In Depth*, by Dick Stout; *Successful Treasure Hunting*, by Lance Comfort; or *The Urban Treasure Hunter*, by Michael Chaplan.

Along the same lines, there are some excellent books out on specializations of metal detecting, such as beach hunting or searching for gold. Again, there are too many to list, but some good examples are *Beach Detecting in Surf & Sand*, by Jay Schofield; *Water Hunting: Secrets of the Pros*, by James Clynick; and *The Complete, Unabridged Zip-Zip*, on gold prospecting by Larry Sallee. The point is, whatever specialty you are interested in probably has a book written about it.

Try shallow water. Most general purpose detectors have waterproof coils (check to be sure before you attempt this), and while water detecting is a specialty art, simple ponds with just a few inches of water are well within the range of the adventurous detectorist.

> "Try detecting the shallow water areas. The reason for this is that many treasure hunters don't like hunting in the water or their coils aren't waterproof."

- Dennis Arendt, *Hit the Treasure Hot Spots*, W&E Treasures, August, 1988.

9. Science and Your Hobby

Science helps you with treasure hunting. You WILL be gaining scientific knowledge, before, during, and after your hunts in the field. You will learn about the weather, soil types, biology, physics, and electronics. All these sciences play a role in your hobby. Best of all, you will learn to enjoy science, as it provides direct help for you in finding treasures.

People often ask "How do coins get buried?" This is a typical question that science answers easily. When water evaporates it turns into a gas; it vaporizes. Normally you cannot see the water in the air, but when conditions are right you can see the moisture in clouds and fog. Water vapor in the air will condense back into liquid form when it comes in contact with a dust particle. Rain includes both the dust and the water. That's why your car windshield is dirty after a rain. Smoke and larger dirt particles come down as soon as the warm air from the fire cools off. Just like the dust particles in rainwater, smoke and soot also land on the ground and on any coins that may have been dropped. Add to that all kinds of natural debris: dead leaves, blown dirt, bird droppings, and you can see how, in a short time, the coin gets covered up. Even meteorites contribute to the mix. Scientists estimate that over 200 tons of meteorite dust lands on the earth every day. The point is, scientific knowledge can explain a lot about how things work - - both in metal detecting and in life in general. Let's take a look at how some different fields of study can help you understand metal detecting.

A. Archeology

Archeologists don't simply dig holes. They learn about the history of what they are looking for. They select a site then painstakingly establish a grid pattern for searching, with strings to mark the borders of each grid square. They record how deep they dig with each level of searching. You can see how such disciplined searching can teach a thing or two to treasure hunters. Such techniques come in handy when you know the site you are searching is going to contain some valuable artifacts.

If this study strikes your fancy, you might want to check out the American Society for Amateur Archeology (http://asaa-persimmonpress.com/). Some helpful books on the subject include *Archaeology Essentials*: Theories, Methods, and Practice (Second Edition), by Colin Renfrew **or *Archaeology For Dummies*** by Nancy Marie White.

Figure 44. Quartz veins (light areas in left photo) running through a rock show where gold is often found. Right: gold panning statue in Auburn, California.

B. Geology

The first thing you'll learn while detecting is the soil type in your area. It may be sandy, loamy, hard-pack clay, or highly mineralized soil. This affects your digging and your detector settings. Soon you'll be tracking where erosion occurs, where sedimentation is covering up coins, and where salt deposits are affecting your detector.

Geology is particularly important in prospecting for gold, as gold often occurs along with quartz, and you will need to learn where the quartz deposits are. Gold is also quite heavy, and will sink to the bedrock. You'll learn to keep an eye out for bedrock outcroppings.

For more information, see the Amateur Geologist website (https://www.amateurgeologist.com/). They feature a series of popular books which you may have seen. They are entitled *Roadside Geology for* (your state), or *Geology Underfoot for* (your state) by various authors. Try also:
The Practical Geologist: The Introductory Guide to the Basics of Geology and to Collecting and Identifying Rocks, by Dougal Dixon.

C. Biology

Every time you dig a hole you will come across insects, worms, larval cocoons, and germinating seeds in the ground. You will start to recognize tree types, vegetation (especially poison oak, poison ivy!), and the birds. You will see tiny trails in the grass where the rodents run, and where the deer wander. You know, it becomes a joy!

The field of biology encompasses vast areas of knowledge, from trees and plants to bugs, birds, and beasts of the field. One of the most rewarding aspects of treasure hunting is having the chance to get out into nature and see all the wildlife. You might enjoy learning the names of birds in your area, or the types of trees. The National Audubon Society has a number of excellent field guides on plants and birds.

Many detecting enthusiasts just love taking field notes of the things they see in nature. If this strikes your fancy, check out *Keeping a Nature Journal*: Discover a Whole New Way of Seeing the World Around You, by Clare Walker Leslie, or *Field Notes on Science & Nature* 1st Edition by Michael R. Canfield.

Figure 45. Estimating the age of a tree will provide clues to how old the search site is. Here a big old stump shows this area has not changed in many years.

D. Meteorology

Funny, but you find yourself watching the weather channel when you are a treasure hunter. You learn about cloud types and which cloud formations forecast rain. You learn that birds sitting on the wires indicates a low pressure system is moving in. You certainly learn to appreciate the wind-chill factor.

For further information, try: *The Weather Identification Handbook*: The Ultimate Guide for Weather Watchers 1st Edition, by Storm Dunlop (his real name!). The National Audubon Society *Field Guide to North American Weather,* by David Ludlum is also recommended.

E. Electronics

Physics, electronics, electromagnetism . . . these are all part and parcel of understanding how your detector works. This is the science of how an electromagnetic field interacts with the ground and with coins. You will learn about coil types, wave patterns, VLF radio frequencies, battery life, and headphone impedance. These are skills that will help you in other areas of your life too.

As with biology, electricity and electronics is a broad science. One of the best places to start is with ham radio's Amateur Radio Relay League (ARRL). They publish a number of books on radio and how circuits work. See, for example, the ***ARRL Ham Radio License Manual***: All You Need to Become an Amateur Radio Operator by the American Radio Relay League.

An understanding of electronics and physics will help you fathom some of the advanced features of metal detectors, such as how cutting edge discrimination works. Some high-end metal detectors, such as the Minelab Explorer series, are capable of measuring both conductivity and resistivity in the target, which adds an entire new dimension to your ability to distinguish junk from valuable finds.

Some good books for learning electricity include:
Basic Electricity: Complete Course, Volumes 1-5 in 1 Revised Edition, by Van Valkenburg, or ***Basic Electricity*** (Dover Books on Electrical Engineering) 2nd Edition, by the Bureau of Naval Personnel.

F. Physical fitness

Being out in the field for hours will improve your health. The doctor might ask you to do 100 deep knee bends a day, and you wouldn't do it, but go out metal detecting and you'll do twice that number in just a short time. You will get more exercise, fresh air, and muscle tone than you'll get at an indoor gym. You'll learn to eat foods that sustain you on a long treasure hunt, and you'll be having fun while gaining stamina.

There are many good books on staying fit, such as *Essentials of Strength Training and Conditioning* 2nd Edition by NSCA - National Strength & Conditioning Association. Just practicing your metal detecting, however, is a major step to staying fit. A metal detecting trip generally takes between two and four hours, in which time you'll walk a few miles. Walking, squatting, and digging are all good exercises.

Figure 46. Hiking trails and metal detecting are a nice fit. Walking builds stamina and helps you appreciate nature. It's enjoyable too!

10. Caring for Your Treasures

A. Coins

1. Rough cleaning

Treat your coins carefully, even as you retrieve them. Most coins are worth only their face value, but as any coin-shooter knows, we find lots of older coins, and plenty of relatively rare ones. These more valuable treasures will lose much of their numismatic value if you have scratches on them made from your digging tools. Even rubbing the dirt off as you hold the coin between your fingers is enough to degrade them with scratches. One of the hardest substances on earth is silica, the main ingredient of sand and sandpaper, and rubbing dirt on the coin will leave visible marks.

Just dust off the coin lightly and put it in your pouch. Some hobbyists carry a plastic bottle with soapy water and put the coins in there to soak until they get home. Once you're back home rinse the dirt off in running water. Many people use one of those kitchen sponges that have a tough plastic scouring pad on them. That plastic will not scratch the metal, and it is good for getting off the loose gunk. Generally, that's all you need to do before storing the coins.

2. Major cleaning

Rule of Thumb: **DO NOT CLEAN YOUR COINS!**
Cleaning will remove the luster and patina that make them
valuable to collectors. Once you've done the basic steps to
remove loose dirt, you should be able to tell whether or
not the coins are valuable. Some collectors, just for the
sake of appearance, like to clean these less valuable coins.

For valuable coins that are dirty, your best bet is to bring them to
a jeweler and soak them in an ultrasonic cleaning machine. This
method is relatively safe. If you are finding many collector value
coins you might even want to buy one of these ultrasonic units,
as the consumer models are under $40.

If you decide you DO want to clean found coins yourself, check
the dates first to remove any that have collector value. For all
other coins, keep the different denominations separate as you
process them. That is, sort them into groups of copper pennies
(prior to 1982), clad pennies, nickels, dimes, and quarters, etc.
Let them soak in white vinegar, each in their own container.
Again, you can use a kitchen sponge with a soft plastic scouring
pad to remove stubborn stains. Sometimes you will have to soak
them for hours. Once clean, give them a thorough rinse in water.
Vinegar is a weak acid that helps remove dirt. It will also remove
the patina on coins, leaving a slightly bleached appearance.

Figure 47. Found coins have stains and tarnish, but cleaning can decrease their value for collectors.

3. Recording and cataloging

Consider keeping a record of the coins you find. Write down the dates of the coins you find, and circle the ones that are earlier than 1965, when dimes and quarters were still made of silver. Then, all you have to do is page through that daily planner looking at the circled entries, and you will see where the best sites are for finding the older coins. Some hobbyists go so far as to keep a record sheet showing a map of where they hunted, for how long, as well as the dates of the coins they find.

Coin collecting is a popular hobby in itself. When you find old and rare coins, you'll want to see what the value is. There are books, magazines, and web sites that can help you assess the value of your collection. Some metal detecting enthusiasts simply throw all their coins into a big jar. Others like to sort and catalog them, so they can add up their total worth. Coin shops sell supplies to make short work of organizing your coins.

Many web pages can help you in your quest for knowledge about coins. See http://en.wikipedia.org/wiki/Coin_collecting. When you are at the bookstore, check out the coin collecting magazines. They will list the current values for most American coins.

Figure 48. Coin shops and metal detecting stores sell all kinds of
materials for storing and organizing your coin finds.

B. Relics

1. The fun of relic hunting

Oh, just wait until the first time you find that cool historic relic! You'll be grinning from ear to ear. There are literally tons of awesome goodies in the ground waiting for you to discover. They range from bullets to buckles, and old toys to timepieces. They are little bits of history that tell you something about the life and times of the people who lived long ago.

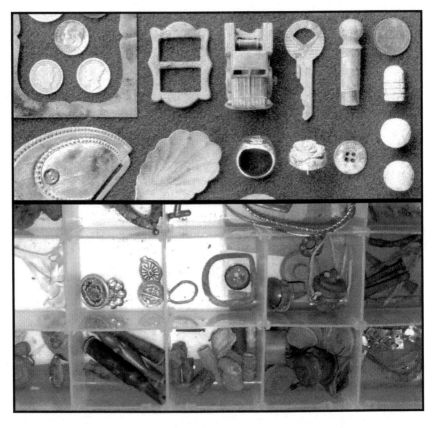

Figure 49. Besides coins you'll find buckles, buttons, bullets, jewelry and other relics. Thanks to Flickr poster Anthony R. from Massachusetts for the top photo.

Figure 50. Valuable coins are often displayed in plastic pocket pages, cardboard coin holders and plastic sleeves.

Many treasure hunters like to specialize in specific types of relics, depending on what is common in the area, and what their interests are. Civil War relic hunters are probably the most popular sub-group. There are also button historians, bottle collectors, toy enthusiasts, and all sorts of sub-specialties in relic hunting. See the following as examples:

- Bottle Collectors Haven: http://www.antiquebottles.com/.
- Virginia Civil War Relics: http://www.virginiarelics.com/.

2. Common relics

Some of the common relics you will find:
- Trade tokens were popular for businesses in the first half of the 20th century. More recent tokens include pressed pennies that are found at tourist sites, arcade game tokens, such as Chuck E. Cheese, and various vending machine tokens.
- Bullets and shell casings are common. You will find bullets from law enforcement, shooting ranges, hunters, military, and even criminal elements. Again, Civil War bullets are prized collector items.
- Buckles range from belt buckles, purse snaps, pajama clips, and horse saddle clasps.
- Buttons were sometimes made of metal. Military and Civil War buttons are important collector items.
- Toys, tin soldiers, costume jewelry
- Household items, including time pieces, nibs from ink pens, broaches, and pins
- Farm and industry items

As with coins, hobbyists have all sorts of standards regarding saving, collecting, and storing their relic finds. There is a brisk business on the internet for people who like to sell or trade the many things they find. In fact, many sellers use the term "metal detector finds" to describe the various and sundry treasures that come their way.

3. Identifying what you've found

Very often you'll find something that you think might be valuable, or interesting, but you cannot tell what it is, or what it was used for. Several of the online forums can be of help here. Simply post a picture and ask your fellow diggers what they think it is. Somewhere in the world is an expert, or at least somebody with a little more experience, who can tell you the identity of your little treasure.

For personal help, check out the TreasureNet forums: http://www.treasurenet.com/forums/. If you post a photo of your finds there you will definitely get help. Look in the antiques section of the bookstore, too, and you will find all kinds of reference materials to help identify things. One great source is the reprinted *1897 Sears, Roebuck Catalogue*, Chelsea House Publishing (facsimile) for relic hunters.

Western and Eastern Treasures magazine has a feature column called "Ask Mark Parker" where he identifies old relics. Be sure to check out current as past issues of the magazine.

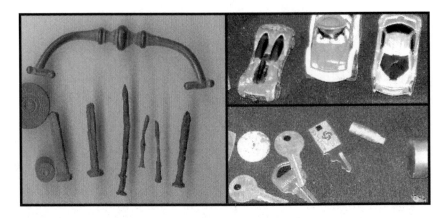

Figure 51. Square nails are a good indication you're digging in an old spot. Modern toys and keys are more recent.

C. Jewelry

Jewelry is a common find in metal detecting. You will find rings, pins, broaches, ear-rings, bracelets and watches. Many of these things can be recycled or given away as gifts. Some detectorists will have precious metal melted down, but you will lose the artistic value of the piece. Others just store the jewelry or make a display out of them. Clean jewelry as you would valuable coins. First use mild soap and water. If necessary, use an ultrasonic cleaning machine. See page 162.

Metal detecting enthusiasts have a strong tradition of trying to locate the owners of wedding rings and engraved jewelry. There is no greater treasure than seeing the look of appreciation on the face of someone who is reunited with his wedding ring or college ring. Such reunions are often covered by the local newspaper, and you can help that happen by notify publishers.

11. Prospecting

Prospecting for our purposes covers searching for metal ores and elements, such as for gold and silver. We also cover searching for meteorites in this chapter.

A. Gold prospecting overview

Gold prospecting can range from a part-time curiosity for a person with a metal detector, to a full blown and distinct hobby in itself with little resemblance to the coin-shooter/treasure hunter that you'll see in a park.

Gold, silver, and other metals can be highly conductive, and display a broad range of readings on the detector display. Gold in particular benefits from a detector with higher operating frequencies. Prospecting will also steer you towards specific, often remote locations, into stream beds, and to abandoned mining areas. These factors combine to nudge the prospecting enthusiast to purchase specialized equipment.

It's true that many metal detectors have a prospecting mode that can be accessed with the simple flip of a switch, but a multiple-mode detector may not always be as well suited to the rigors of the dedicated gold prospector. The curious detectorist has at least a chance of finding microscopic traces of gold, and even an occasional nugget, but to move into the major leagues, you will need to join groups that have access to private land claims, and field trips to known gold sites.

Figure 52. Gold if found using different types of equipment, such as the sluice box shown here.

Hunting for gold is a different kind of experience, and requires different skills.

"Nugget hunting differs from coin-shooting. Coins are large compared to most nuggets. A one grain bit of gold is smaller than a match head and will cause a very light signal. The nugget hunter must listen for faint sounds caused by very small objects and he must train his ears for those sounds. The soil where gold is found is usually highly mineralized, so it is essential to follow the operating manual directions for tuning and ground balancing your machine."

- Dorothy B. Francis, *Metal Detecting for Treasure*

172

Many gold prospectors do not use a metal detector at all, but prefer to use gold panning techniques. This involves swishing sand around in a pan and spinning out the lighter elements. The heavier, gold laden remains are further sifted to enable you to pick out the gold flakes. Using sluices and gold dredges, likewise, do not use metal detectors.

If you are interesting in exploring gold prospecting, then consider:

The Gold Prospecting Association
Internet: http://www.goldprospectors.org/
Magazine: ***Gold Prospectors***
Group: Gold Prospectors Association of America, P.O. Box 891509, Tumecula, CA 92589. The association membership is separate from the magazine subscription.

You would benefit from looking at books that specialize in this subject, such as:

Recreational Gold Prospecting for Fun & Profit by Gail Butler and Paul D. Morrison (Paperback - May 1998)

Gold! Gold! How and Where to Prospect for Gold by Joseph F. Petralia, Jill Applegate, and Susan Neri (Paperback - 2006)

You Can Find Gold: With a Metal Detector by Charles Garrett and Roy Lagal (Paperback - November 1995)

B. Gold locating equipment

Since gold and silver are heavier than most rocks, they will often settle to the bottom of streams and areas where erosion has occurred. To get at it requires digging, and if this occurs in a stream there are different methods of extracting the valuable ores. Dredges, sluice boxes, and rocker boxes are tools that may be affordable for amateur prospectors, though prices can range into the thousands of dollars as the equipment gets more sophisticated. Again, gold dredging is a specialized topic. It may be too advanced to cover fully in a general metal detecting book.

Gold also settles in cracks and crevices of bedrock, giving rise to specialized handheld equipment, such as gold probes and picks that can ferret out the fine particles.

C. Silver

Silver occurs in veins, just like gold. It is more difficult to identify silver than gold, as it is easily mixed up with lead or other grayish minerals. Silver will show up along a broad range of values on a discriminating detector, depending on its purity. The best bet if you think you've found a silver nugget is to bring it home and test it at a later time. The metal detecting supply stores and internet sites sell a silver testing kit to determine if you really do have silver. The test kit uses 10% nitric acid; if the sample turns black, it is silver. This kit is handy to have for found jewelry too, as sometimes silver jewelry may be difficult to distinguish from base metals.

174

D. Meteorites

Hunting for meteorites is a particular form of metal detecting that is both interesting and potentially valuable. Finding meteorites is rare. Most people who are searching for meteorites start with research into areas that have a high probability of yielding some success. The best places to hunt are in locations that have been identified as "strewn fields" – areas where a meteorite fragments have been found in the past.

Meteorites are naturally occurring objects that originate in space and survive a fall to the ground through the atmosphere. Most are remnants of asteroids or possibly comets.
http://meteorite.org/

> "It may seem fairly obvious, but it is still worth saying: the easiest way to find a meteorite is to go where they have been found before. A **strewn field** is a zone where multiple meteorites from the same fall have been recovered. There are many strewn fields around the world, and several here in the United States. One of the best known is Holbrook in northern Arizona."

- http://geology.com/meteorites/meteorite-hunting.shtml

There are several different kinds of meteorites, and not all are readily identified. Once you find a particular candidate, you have to subject the rock to a number of tests to solidify its identity.

> "Some of the common clues to look for are rocks that are magnetic, and have a fusion crust on the surface caused by heat when the meteorite entered the earth's atmosphere."

- Lance Downing, *Rocks from Outer Space*, Lost Treasures, November, 2004.

The easiest to identify are nickel-iron meteorites, as they are magnetic, very dense and heavy for their size, and often have particular physical markings.

Meteorites have several distinct features you can use to identify them. Sometimes, however a more detailed chemical analysis may be required.

Look for:

- A fusion crust; a darkened outer layer
- Regmaglypts, which are thumbprint-like indentations
- High density
- Magnetic attraction
- High Iron-nickel content
- Chondrules; round grains.

You can find meteorites with most detectors made for finding coins and jewelry. Most meteorites are small, but some can range to boulder-sized megaliths. This prompts some enterprising detectorists to favor larger coils or cache detectors. This quickly leads to very specialized detecting, which goes beyond the scope of this book.

12. Mastering Metal Detecting

Once you've learned the basics of metal detecting, it's time to grow into the sport, in order to gain the maximum pleasure and rewards from your adventures. Let's look at some ways to work up to the next level.

A. Contributing and participating

There's a saying that "Friends multiply your joys and divide your sorrows." That's especially true for the people you'll meet at your local detecting club. Club meetings are a great place for:

- Sharing stories about your hunting trips
- Learning new techniques, learning from the pros and old-timers
- Teaching people who have less experience than yourself
- Finding bargains on metal detecting equipment
- Discovering good places to hunt
- Participating in contests and group hunts
- Meeting new friends
- Expanding your scope of activities

One of the best ways to contribute to the sport is to join with others or join a club and share your experiences. You might find that you are attracted to detecting specialties, such as finding relics, or shallow water detecting. These are important skills that have great value for newcomers. Teaching others is a real joy.

Another favorite is to try to find the owners of the rings that you find. There is a tradition in metal detecting of attempting to locate the owners of lost jewelry. This requires some detective work, and it generally requires that the ring have an inscription on the inside.

You will find that after a while you really get to know the intricacies of your detector. You learn how to tune it up for your ground conditions and how recognize sounds and discrimination readings. Again, this is knowledge that is fun to share with people who own the same equipment.

B. Online forums and reviews

Once you've gotten your feet wet in this sport – sometimes literally – you can more fully participate in the many online discussions available on the internet forum web sites. You can tell others your experience with your brand of detector, and even write product reviews. You will soon become a fully engaged member of the online community. This is both a learning and a teaching experience that helps you stretch and grow, and it's a benefit to others too.

Look at all the time you spent deciding what detector to buy, and the hours you spent learning to tweak the dials. Isn't that experience valuable to people who just bought the same detector? Go online and share your rapidly increasing knowledge.

The online forums and the people you meet at club meetings are a valuable resource that you will need when you decide to move up to a more expensive detector.

C. Review your early choices

After you've gone on several hunts, take a few minutes to look back and re-evaluate some of your early decisions. Is the detector working the way you expected? Is that coil too heavy for your enjoyment? Is it time to buy some decent digging tools? Rather than getting into a rut that detracts from the fun, make an honest assessment of what is right and what is wrong with what you're using so far.

Apply that same evaluation process to your selection of hunting sites. Are they paying off? Would some library research improve your take-home haul? Maybe you liked going out alone, but now you find having a companion or two along with you is more enjoyable. Fellow hunters can help you improve your hunting and digging techniques, and can think of places to search you may not have thought of.

Finally, take another look at the sciences that might help you in your search for treasures. Maybe that book on geology will come in handy when you decide to look for gold nuggets. Maybe that article on ground balancing will help you adjust your detector for maximum performance.

This sport is an ongoing adventure. If you want to keep it fresh and inspiring, don't be afraid to change your mind and trek off in a new direction.

D. Top ten tips for mastery

This is an admittedly biased (editor's choice) list of the top ten things you can do to improve your metal detecting.

1. Buy a good hand-held probe. A quality pin-pointer, such as the White's Bullseye Probe, or the Garrett Pro Pointer, will speed up discovery of coins and jewelry once your detector spots it. Often you can locate the target with the probe even before you start digging. A good probe will cut coin retrieval time by more than half.
2. Develop good coil swinging technique. Keep the coil close to the ground and parallel to the surface. There is a tendency to lift the coil up at the extremes of the swing. This reduces the effective depth of detection.
3. Use a grid system to search an area.
4. Consider multiple coils of different sizes for different places.
5. Re-read your detector user manual.
6. Spend time researching the best hunt areas.
7. Join a metal detecting club.
8. Stay informed. Read metal detecting magazines and watch metal detecting videos online.
9. Be kind to the Earth. Hasn't she been good to you?
10. Give yourself a yearly self-assessment of what you like and dislike about metal detecting. Then make changes to suit.

Appendix A: Metal Detecting Resources

A. The big players

The following are some of the big players in treasure hunting, as they combine a magazine and a major World Wide Web presence.

TreasureNet
Internet: http://www.treasurenet.com/
Forum: http://forum.treasurenet.com/index.php

Lost Treasure
Internet: http://www.losttreasure.com/
Magazine: *Lost Treasure*
Mail: LostTreasure®, Box 451589, Grove, OK 74345-1589
SubscriptionL LostTreasure®, P.O. Box 469091, Escondido, CA 92046

Gold Prospector's Association
Internet: http://www.goldprospectors.org/
Magazine: *Gold Prospectors*
Group: Gold Prospectors Association of America, P.O. Box 891509, Tumecula, CA 92589.

B. Magazines

Western & Eastern Treasures
People's Publishing
P.O. Box 37
Sausalito, CA 94965
(415) 339-0124

Lost Treasure
LostTreasure
P.O. Box 469091
Escondido, CA 92046
(866) 469-6224

Gold Prospectors
Gold Prospectors Association of America
43445 Business Park Drive Suite #113
Temecula, CA 92590 (800) 551-9707

American Digger
American Digger
P.O. Box 126
Aeworth, GA 3101
(770) 362-8671

ICMJ's Prospecting and Mining Journal
ICMJ
PO Box 2260
Aptos, CA 95001
(831) 479-1500

C. Online resources

These are the top metal detecting Internet sites, roughly in order by popularity:

- TreasureNet: http://www.treasurenet.com
- The Friendly Metal Detecting Forum: http://metaldetectingforum.com/index.php
- Kellyco: http://www.kellycodetectors.com/indexmain.php
- Lost Treasure On Line: http://www.losttreasure.com
- Find's Treasure Forums: http://www.findmall.com/
- White's Electronics Forum: http://forums.whiteselectronics.com/forum.php
- Treasure Depot: http://www.thetreasuredepot.com/index.html
- Treasure Quest: http://www.treasurequestxlt.com/
- Treasure Spot: http://www.mytreasurespot.com/
- American Detectorist http://www.americandetectorist.com/
- Big Boys Hobbies: http://forum.bigboyshobbies.net/
- Metal Detector Reviews: http://metaldetectorreviews.net/
- Metal Detecting World: http://metaldetectingworld.com/ Foreign:
- OKM, Germany: http://www.okmmetaldetectors.com/
- UK and European Metal Detecting Forum; http://www.metaldetectingforum.co.uk/ Coins:
- Coinflation – (silver coin melt value): http://www.coinflation.com/coins/silver_coin_calculator. html
- Coin World: http://www.coinworld.com/

For **video** try YouTube or Google videos and type in "metal detecting." That will keep you entertained for quite a while! Many of the videos are instructional in nature.

D. Clubs

The Federation of Metal Detector and Archaeological Clubs
http://www.fmdac.org/

World Wide Association of Treasure Seekers
http://www.wwats.org/

2. Lists of local clubs

For a club in your local area, see any of the links below. You can also try a search on the internet using the keywords of your home town and the words "metal detecting club."

- Go Metal Detecting:
  http://gometaldetecting.com/links-clubs.htm
- Kelly Co.
  http://www.kellycodetectors.com/clubs/
- DMOZ Open Directory
  http://www.dmoz.org/Recreation/Outdoors/Metal_Detecting/Organizations/.
- Friendly Forum
  http://metaldetectingforum.com/showthread.php?t=14013.

E. Further reading

1. Books on metal detecting

Metal Detecting: A Beginner's Guide: to Mastering the Greatest Hobby In the World *by Mark Smith, January, 2014*

Metal Detecting for the Beginner, 2nd Edition. by Vince Migliore, May, 2010.

Metal Detecting for Beginners and Beyond by Tim Kerber, August, 2014.

Metal Detecting the Beach by Mark D. Smith, February, 2013.

How to Research for Treasure Hunting and Metal Detecting: From Lead Generation to Vetting by Otto Von Helsing, January, 2013.

Gold Beneath the Waves: Treasure Hunting the Surf and Sand by Jim F. Brouwer, Jan 19, 2012.

The Urban Treasure Hunter: A Practical Handbook for Beginners by Michael Chaplan. (Paperback, 2004.)

2. Articles and papers

Before You Buy That Metal Detector (Online article by Lee Wiese): http://www.mdhtalk.org/articles/metal-detector-decision/metal-detector-decision.htm.

3. Handy reference books

Antique Tool Collectors Guide to Value, by Ronald S. Barlow (Paperback - 1999).

Collecting Costume Jewelry 101: The Basics of Starting, Building and Upgrading (Identification & Value Guide) by Julia C. Carroll (Paperback - 2004).

Collector's Illustrated Encyclopedia of the American Revolution, George C. Neumann.

1897 Sears, Roebuck Catalogue, Chelsea House Publishing (facsimile; for relic hunters).

2015 U.S. Coin Digest: The Complete Guide to Current Market Values (Us Coin Digest) by David C. Harper and Harry S. Miller, yearly editions.

Antique Iron: Identification and Values, by Kathryn McNerney (Paperback – 1983).

Civil War Collector's Price Guide, by Nancy Rossbacher, (Paperback – 2010).

Standard Catalog of US Tokens, by Russell Rulau, (Paperback - September, 2004).

F. Friends and neighbors

Reminder: Your best resource for finding treasures is the people around you. Be sure to talk to neighbors, friends, family members, librarians, and historians about your interest in metal detecting. Very often older folks have stories and insight into places people congregated, or when they held outdoor social events. This is a tremendously valuable resource. All it takes is a little friendly hello, and you can steer the conversation into a discussion of your hobby. You'll be surprised how helpful and cooperative people can be.

> **Hint:** Some treasure hunters make up a simple business card describing what they do, and have that card ready for impromptu meetings with people. Some will even carry around a few old coins to get the conversation started.

Appendix B: How a Detector Works

A. VLF technology

Take a penny, a nickel, and a dime. One by one, drop them on a desk. You'll notice each one has a distinctive clunk or clank as it bounces off the surface. With a little practice you'd soon be able to learn which coin is being dropped, even without looking. The same kind of thing happens electronically when a coin is hit with radio frequency radiation. Each coin produces a specific electronic signature which the detector can recognize. Similarly, other common items, like pull tabs, or bottle caps, have their own unique responses. Unfortunately, some common junk items have responses that are pretty close to those of valuable coins, so the detector doesn't always get it right.

The most popular instrumentation in use today is the Very Low Frequency (VLF) detector. It uses two coils, one for transmitting and the other for receiving a signal back from the search area. The receive coil is close to the transmit coil, usually concentric but smaller in size. The effects of the transmitted energy are cancelled out by running a voltage in the receiver windings in the opposite direction from the transmit coil. This balances out the magnetic field in the receive coil, which is why it is sometimes called balanced induction technology. This balancing act means any signal the receive coil detects comes from objects in the ground, rather than from the transmit coil.

The metal detector contains an oscillator, which produces an alternating current (AC) in the transmit coil. Whenever current flows in a wire it creates a magnetic field around the wire. An AC current in this coil means the current first runs in one direction, builds up to a peak, then decreases again towards zero, and repeats the same pattern in the opposite direction. The rise and fall of the voltage occurs in accordance with electrical principles to form a sine wave. Alternating current in a straight wire creates a magnetic field around it, perpendicular to the wire. When the wire is formed into the loops of the coil, this magnetic field becomes concentrated in the center of the coil, again, perpendicular to the axis of the coil. The magnetic field strength increases and decreases in time with the sine wave voltage. This means the magnetic field is continually growing then decreasing around the coil, and forms the search area of the coil.

When such a moving field encounters a metallic object, it generates a current in that object, be it a coin, or a nail, or a bottle cap. At least, the magnetic field *tries* to create a current. Some metals, such as iron, are **resistive** to being influenced by the magnetic field. This is called ferromagnetic resistance. Other metals, such as silver, are **conductive.** They have lots of loose electrons which respond quickly to changes in the magnetic field. When the field from the coil moves across a coin in the ground, the field generates a small current in the coin. This current, in turn, creates it own magnetic field, which pushes back on the coil's field, causing a phase shift. See Figure 53.

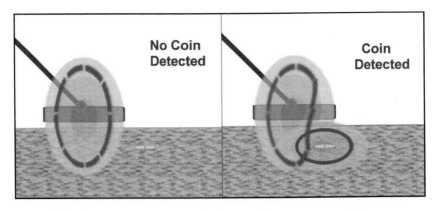

Figure 53. The field from the detector's coil induces a current in the coin which then pushes back on the coil field, causing a phase shift.

The response of the target to the magnetic wave is a result of the composition of the target. It creates a **phase shift** in the received

188

signal. Every coin or piece of metal displays some mixture of resistive and conductive properties. That mixture, the ratio of resistive to conductive makeup, will have a specific response, or signature, as picked up by the receiving coil. This enables the detector to discriminate between a coin and a piece of junk. The size of the scanned object will determine the amplitude, or loudness of the received signal. The phase shift will determine the probable composition. These two bits of information help identify the target.

The output is generally fed to a meter, called a Visual Discrimination Indicator (VDI), or Target Identification (TID) circuitry, which will display a number or give a name to the target. This helps the treasure hunter decide whether to dig the target or not. Many detectors assign a number corresponding with the VDI readout. On the White's MXT metal detector, for example, the VDI for a dime might be 80, while a nickel appears as 18. After a period of working with one detector, the operator quickly learns what the numbers are for different coins and for pull-tabs.

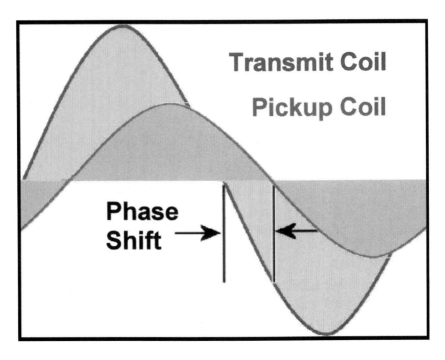

Transmit Coil

Pickup Coil

Phase Shift →   ←

Figure 54. The composition of the target determines the phase shift in the receiver coil, smaller waveform.

Target Identification is not always accurate. Deeper targets and coins sitting on edge are more difficult to identify. Pull tabs and other asymmetrical targets will sometimes give mixed signals depending on how you approach them. If your coil is scanning East-West, for example, a pull tab might show up as a nickel. Then when you scan it North-South it will register as a pull-tab.

B. Pulse Induction (PI) technology

Pulse Induction detectors use a short burst of energy to create a magnetic field around the coil. When the burst terminates, the magnetic field collapses, generating a spike of power in the coil in the opposite direction. The waveforms in electronics circuits are precise and uniform, so this rebound spike is exactly the same in power content from cycle to cycle. The energy from the spike is measured by passing it through a resistive-capacitive circuit, which measures exactly how long it takes to discharge.

If a coin is present, the coin will generate a much smaller field from the eddy currents induced by the original pulse. The target then adds a minute amount of energy to that power spike. The amount time it takes to discharge, then, is ever so slightly different. A crude analogy is to think of a bucket with a nail hole in the bottom. If you pour exactly one cup of water in the pail, it might take 5 seconds to drain out. If you pour one cup plus one ounce of water, it might take 5.1 seconds to drain out. The change in the discharge time indicates the presence of a target.

The advantage of PI detectors is that they do a great job of detecting in mineralized soil or beach sand. The downside is that many objects produce similar amounts of feedback energy, so that discriminating between a piece of junk and a coin is not as acute as the induction-balance (VLF) detector.

Appendix C:
Manufacturers and Suppliers

A. Major brands

The major brand metal detector manufacturers generally sell detectors for land based coin, jewelry and treasure hunting, as well as specialty detectors for prospecting or underwater searching. They often sell supplies and peripherals for hobbyists.

In alphabetical order:

Bounty Hunter
1465 Henry Brennan Dr # H
El Paso, TX 79936
(915) 633-8354   (800) 444-5994
Web: http://www.detecting.com/
Bounty Hunter sells its products through major retailers, such as The Bounty Hunter Store (http://www.BountyHunterStore.com), and Kellyco, (http://www.kellycodetectors.com).

Garrett Electronics
1881 W. State Street
Garland, TX 75042
Tel: (972) 494-6151   Fax: (972) 494-1881
Web: http://www.garrett.com/
Email: sales@garrett.com
Garret has a large security division in addition to the hobby division. Charles Garrett has written several books on metal detecting.

Fisher Labs
1465-H Henry Brennan
El Paso, TX 79936
Tel: (915) 225-0333   Fax: (915) 225-0336
Web: http://www.fisherlab.com/hobby/index.html
Email: info@fisherlab.com
Fisher Labs has three divisions, hobby, industrial, and security.

JW Fishers Mfg Inc
1953 County Street
East Taunton, MA 02718
Tel: (800) 822-4744
Web: http://www.jwfishers.com/
Email: Info@jwfishers.com

Minelab USA
871 Grier Dr., Suite B1
Las Vegas, NV 89119 USA
Tel: (702) 891-8809   Fax: (702) 891-8810
Web: http://www.minelab.com/usa/consumer
Email: info@minelabusa.com

Teknetics
1465-H Henry Brennan
El Paso, TX 79936
Tel: 1-800-413-4131
Web: http://www.tekneticst2.com/

Tesoro Electronics
715 White Spar Road
Prescott, AZ 86303
Tel: (928) 771-2646
Web: http://www.tesoro.com/
Email: support @ tesoro.com

White's Electronics
1011 Pleasant Valley Road
Sweet Home, OR 97386
Tel: (800) 547-6911
Fax: (541) 367-6629
White's also has regional offices around the US: See
http://whiteselectronics.com/ for local offices and suppliers.

B. Sample prices: MSRP and street price

Below is a selected list of coin/relic metal detectors, in alphabetical order by manufacturer. Just a few gold prospecting and beach/underwater machines are listed for comparison, (G = Gold) and (W = Water). Listings show recent advertised price.

For an up-to-date list of evaluations and street prices, try Metal Detector Reviews, (online at http://metaldetectorreviews.net/), or look at the ratings given by Kellyco, (http://www.kellycodetectors.com/indexmain.php), or any of the other online review sites.

Bounty Hunter – Highest Ratings

Bounty Hunter		Rank
Price	Model	Ratings
$210	Pioneer 202	1
$195	Discovery 3300	2
$110	Discovery 1100	3
$172	Timeranger	4
$190	Quickdraw II	5
$90	Tracker IV	6
$54	GoldDigger	7
$170	Sharpshooter II	8
$293	Landstar	9
$133	Quicksilver	10
$41	Junior BHJS	11
$118	Lonestar	12
$300	Pioneer 505	13
$120	Pioneer EX	14

Appendix Table 1. Bounty Hunter ratings rank.

Bounty Hunter – Number of Reviews

Bounty Hunter		Rank
Price	Model	Reviews
$54	GoldDigger	1
$41	Junior BHJS	2
$90	Tracker IV	3
$133	Quicksilver	4
$170	Sharpshooter II	5
$172	Timeranger	6
$195	Discovery 3300	7
$118	Lonestar	8
$110	Discovery 1100	9
$190	Quickdraw II	10
$300	Pioneer 505	11
$210	Pioneer 202	12
$293	Landstar	13
$120	Pioneer EX	14

Appendix Table 2. Bounty Hunter number of reviews rank.

Fisher – Highest Ratings

Fisher		Rank
Price	Model	Ratings
$505	F5	1
$810	CZ 3D	2
$665	F70	3
$765	Gold Bug 2 (G)	4
$215	F2	5
$680	1280x Aquanaut (W)	6
$950	F75	7
$430	F4	8

Appendix Table 3. Fisher ratings rank.

Fisher – Number of Reviews

Fisher		Rank
Price	Model	Reviews
$215	F2	1
$950	F75	2
$810	CZ 3D	3
$430	F4	4
$505	F5	5
$765	Gold Bug 2 (G)	6
$665	F70	7
$680	1280x Aquanaut (W)	8

Appendix Table 4. Fisher number of reviews rank.
(G) = Gold. (W) = Water.

Garrett – Highest Ratings

Garrett		Rank
Price	Model	Ratings
$300	Ace 350	1
$680	AT Gold (G)	2
$212	Ace 250	3
$155	Ace 150	4
$1,065	Infinium LS (W)	5
$935	GTI 2500	6
$600	AT Pro (W)	7

Appendix Table 5. Garrett ratings rank.
(G) = Gold. (W) = Water.

Garrett – Number of Reviews

Garrett		Rank
Price	Model	Reviews
$212	Ace 250	1
$155	Ace 150	2
$600	AT Pro (W)	3
$935	GTI 2500	4
$300	Ace 350	5
$1,065	Infinium LS (W)	6
$680	AT Gold (G)	7

Appendix Table 6. Garrett number of reviews rank.
(G) = Gold. (W) = Water.

Minelab – Highest Ratings

Minelab		Rank
Price	Model	Ratings
$1,115	Safari	1
$300	Xterra 305	2
$1,200	Explorer SE	3
$1,200	Excalibur 1000 (W)	4
$1,000	Eureka Gold (G)	5

Appendix Table 7. Minelab ratings rank.
(G) = Gold. (W) = Water.

Minelab – Number of Reviews

Minelab		Rank
Price	Model	Reviews
$1,200	Excalibur 1000 (W)	1
$1,000	Eureka Gold (G)	2
$1,115	Safari	3
$300	Xterra 305	4
$1,200	Explorer SE	5

Appendix Table 8. Minelab number of reviews rank.
(G) = Gold. (W) = Water.

Teknetics – Highest Ratings

Teknetics		Rank
Price	Model	Ratings
$220	EuroTek Pro	1
$250	Delta 4000	2
$900	T2	3

Appendix Table 9. Teknetics ratings rank.

Teknetics – Number of Reviews

Teknetics		Rank
Price	Model	Reviews
$250	Delta 4000	1
$900	T2	2
$220	EuroTek Pro	3

Appendix Table 10. Teknetics number of reviews rank.

Tesoro – Highest Ratings

Tesoro		Rank
Price	Model	Ratings
$555	Outlaw	1
$260	Silver uMax	2
$160	Compadre	3
$680	Lobo SuperTRAQ (G)	4
$450	Vaquero	5
$365	Cibola	6
$600	Tejon	7
$510	DeLeon	8
$580	Sand Shark (W)	9
$725	Cortes	10

Appendix Table 11. Tesoro number of reviews rank.
(G) = Gold. (W) = Water.

Tesoro – Number of Reviews

Tesoro		Rank
Price	Model	Reviews
$365	Cibola	1
$160	Compadre	2
$260	Silver uMax	3
$450	Vaquero	4
$600	Tejon	5
$680	Lobo SuperTRAQ (G)	6
$580	Sand Shark (W)	7
$725	Cortes	8
$510	DeLeon	9
$555	Outlaw	10

Appendix Table 12. Tesoro number of reviews rank.
(G) = Gold. (W) = Water.

Whites – Highest Ratings

Whites		Rank
Price	Model	Ratings
$1,100	Spectra Vx3,	1
$800	MXT Tracker	2
$640	Matrix M6	3
$825	Surf PI (W)	4
$825	MXT All Pro	5
$180	Coinmaster	6
$280	Coinmaster Pro	7
$915	BeachHunter 300 (W)	8

Appendix Table 13. Whites ratings rank.
(W) = Water.

Whites – Number of Reviews

Whites		Rank
Price	Model	Reviews
$800	MXT Tracker	1
$640	Matrix M6	2
$180	Coinmaster	3
$280	Coinmaster Pro	4
$1,100	Spectra Vx3,	5
$915	BeachHunter 300 (W)	6
$825	Surf PI (W)	7
$825	MXT All Pro	8

Appendix Table 14. Whites number of reviews rank.
(W) = Water.

C. Suppliers

Suppliers, in alphabetical order:

Aardvark Metal Detectors (Distributor)
1085 Belle Avenue
Winter Springs, FL 32708
Web: http://www.aardvarkdetectors.com
Email: sales@aardvarkdetectors.com
Tel: (800) 828-1455

Accurate Locators (Manufacturer)
1383 2nd Ave.
Gold Hill, Oregon 97525
Tel: (877) 808-6200
Web: Web: http://www.accuratelocators.com/

DetectorPro (Distributor)
Web: http://www.detectorpro.com/
Email: info@detectorpro.com
Distributor for Headhunter metal detectors and "innovative treasure hunting concepts."

Doc's Detecting Supply (Distributor)
3740 S. Royal Crest Street
Las Vegas, Nevada 89119
Web: http://www.docsdetecting.com/
Email: cop704@yahoo.com
Tel: (800) 477-3211 Ext. 14
Distributor for Coiltek brand coils for Minelab detectors.

Famous Treasures (Distributor)
Tampa Florida
4312 Land o' Lakes
Land O' Lakes, FL 34639
Toll Free (888) 788-1819
(813) 996-1787
Email: sales@famoustreasures.com
Website: http://www.famoustreasures.com/

Jimmy Sierra Products (Accessories)
James and Jim Normandi
6880 Sir Francis Drake Blvd. (P.O. Box 519)
Forest Knolls, California 94933
Telephone: 1-800-457-0875
Website: http://www.jimmysierra.com/
Contact: jimmysierra.com/ask_jimmy_form.htm

JW Fishers Manufacturing (Manufacturer)
1953 County Streets
East Taunton, MA 02718
Web: http://www.jwfishers.com/
Email: info@jwfishers.com
Underwater detectors - Note: Different from Fisher Labs.

Kellyco (Distributor)
1085 Belle Ave
Winter Springs, FL 32708
Tel: (888) 535-5926
Web: http://www.kellycodetectors.com/indexmain.php
Email: orderdept@kellycodetectors.com

Note: Kellyco and other "superstore" distributors carry lesser-known brands and specialty items such as:

Automax (Pinpointing probe)
Link:
http://www.kellycodetectors.com/vibra/automaxprecisionpin
pointer.htm
Cobra (Metal detector manufacturer)
Link: http://www.kellycodetectors.com/cobra/cobramain.htm
MP Digital (Metal detector manufacturer)
Link:
http://www.kellycodetectors.com/MP3/MP3information.htm
Nautilus (Metal detector manufacturer)
Link: http://www.kellycodetectors.com/nautilus/nautilus.htm
Nokta Engineering
Link: http://www.kellycodetectors.com/nokta/nokta_buy.htm
Pioneer (Bounty Hunter)
Link:
http://www.kellycodetectors.com/bountyhunter/pioneer_main
.htm
Teknetics (Metal detector manufacturer)
Link:
http://www.kellycodetectors.com/Teknetics/teknetics.htm
Titan (Metal detectors)
Link: http://www.kellycodetectors.com/titan/titan.htm
Viper (Metal detector manufacturer)
Link:
http://www.kellycodetectors.com/cobra/vipersmain2.htm

Outdoor Outfitters (Distributor)
705 Elm Street,
Waukesha WI 53186
Web: http://www.outdoorout.com/
Email: Outdoorout@ameritech.net
Tel: (800) 558 2020
Fax: 262 542 4435

Predator Tools (Digging tools)
35 South Woodruff Road
Bridgetown, NJ 08302
Web: http://www.predatortools.com/
Web: sales@predatortools.com
Tel: 856-455-3790
Fax: 856-455-6604

Simmons Scientific Products (Locating rods)
P.O. Box 10057
Wilmington, NC 28404
Web: http://www.simmonsscientificproducts.com/
Email: simmonssp@aol.com
Tel. & Fax: (910) 686-1656

Sunray Detector Electronics (In-line target probes, distributor)
106 N Main Street
P.O. Box 300
Hazleton, Iowa 50641-0300
Web: http://www.sunraydetector.com/
Email: infor@sunraydetector.com
Tel: (319) 636-2244

Appendix D: Purchase Check-list Chart

	1. ___	2. ___	3. ___
Street Price			
Discrimination			
Notch Filter			
Sensitivity			
Target ID			
Coil size(s)			
Interchangeable Coil			
Ground Balance			
Operating Frequency(s)			
Weight			
Other: ___			
Other: ___			
Other: ___			
Other: ___			
Reviews – Positive			
Reviews – Negative			
Summary			

Appendix Table 15. Detector comparison check list: Fill in the chart for the top three models in your price range.

Index

Vince Migliore has written several articles on metal detecting, some for *Western & Eastern Treasures* magazine. He is a writer and researcher living in California. He is author of the following books:

- Metal Detecting for the Beginner, March, 2009
- Metal Detecting for the Beginner, 2nd Edition, May, 2010
- Photo Intro to Metal Detecting, June, 2010
- Creative Cache Containers for Geocaching June, 2012
- Geocaching: Basic Beginner's Guide, October, 2013.

<u>Notes</u>

59246017R10122

Made in the USA
San Bernardino, CA
03 December 2017